'Utterly accessible, deeply
humane and startlingly original –
a potent democratic tool
at the perfect time'

NAOMI KLEIN

AUTHOR OF *NO IS NOT ENOUGH*

TALKING TO MY DAUGHTER
ABOUT THE ECONOMY

*Adults in the Room: My Battle with Europe's
Deep Establishment*

*And The Weak Suffer What They Must?: Europe,
Austerity and the Threat to Global Stability*

*The Global Minotaur: America, Europe and the
Future of the Global Economy*

YANIS VAROUFAKIS

Talking to My Daughter About the Economy

A Brief History of Capitalism

TRANSLATED BY
JACOB MOE AND YANIS VAROUFAKIS

THE BODLEY HEAD
LONDON

1 3 5 7 9 10 8 6 4 2

The Bodley Head, an imprint of Vintage,
20 Vauxhall Bridge Road,
London SW1V 2SA

The Bodley Head is part of the Penguin Random House group of companies
whose addresses can be found at global.penguinrandomhouse.com.

Penguin
Random House
UK

First published by Patakis Publishers in the original Greek in 2013
First published in English by The Bodley Head with revisions in 2017

www.penguin.co.uk/vintage

A CIP catalogue record for this book is available from the British Library

Hardback ISBN 9781847924445
Trade paperback ISBN 9781847924421

Typeset in India by Integra Software Services Pvt. Ltd, Pondicherry

Printed and bound by Clays Ltd, St Ives plc

Penguin Random House is committed to a sustainable future for
our business, our readers and our planet. This book is made from
Forest Stewardship Council® certified paper.

MIX
Paper from
responsible sources
FSC® C018179
FSC
www.fsc.org

Contents

Prologue   1

1 Why So Much Inequality?   7

2 The Birth of the Market Society   27

3 The Marriage of Debt and Profit   51

4 The Black Magic of Banking   65

5 Two Oedipal Markets   91

6 Haunted Machines   109

7 The Dangerous Fantasy of
   Apolitical Money   135

8 Stupid Viruses?   165

Epilogue   185

Index   201

Prologue

This book grew out of my Greek publisher's invitation, back in 2013, to talk directly to young people about the economy. My reason for writing it was the conviction that the economy is too important to leave to the economists.

If we want to build a bridge, better to leave it to the experts, to the engineers. If we need surgery, better to find a surgeon to operate. But books that popularize science are important in a world where the president of the United States wages open war against it and our children eschew science courses. Cultivating a broad public appreciation of science throws a protective shield around the scientific community that must produce the experts society needs. In this sense, the small volume here is quite different from those books.

As a teacher of economics, I have always believed that if you are not able to explain the economy in a language young people can understand, then, quite simply, you are clueless yourself. With time, I recognized something else, a delicious contradiction about my own profession that reinforced this belief: *the more scientific our models of the economy become, the less relation they bear to the real, existing economy out there.* This is precisely the opposite of what obtains in physics, engineering and the rest of the real sciences, where increasing scientific sophistication throws more and more light on how nature actually works.

This is why this book is my attempt to do the opposite of popularizing economics: if it succeeds, it should incite its readers to take the economy in their own hands and make them realize that to understand the economy they also have to understand why the self-appointed experts on the economy, the economists, are almost always wrong. Ensuring that everyone is allowed to talk authoritatively about the economy is a prerequisite for a good society and a precondition for an authentic democracy. The economy's ups and downs determine our lives; its forces make a mockery of our democracies; its tentacles reach deep into our souls, where they shape our hopes and aspirations. If we defer to the experts on the economy, we effectively hand to them *all* decisions that matter.

There was another reason I agreed to write this book. My daughter Xenia is an almost constant absence in my life. Living as she does in Australia and I in Greece, we are either far apart or, when we are together, counting the days until the next separation. Talking as if to her about things that the scarcity of time never allowed us to discuss felt good.

Writing the book was a joy. It is the only text I have written without any footnotes, references or the paraphernalia of academic or political books. Unlike those 'serious' books, I wrote it in my native tongue. In fact, I just sat down at our island home in Aegina, overlooking the Saronic Gulf and the mountains of the Peloponnese in the distance, and let the book write itself – without a plan or provisional table of contents or blueprint to guide me. It took nine days, punctuated by the odd swim, boat ride or evening out with Danae, my forgiving and ridiculously supportive partner.

A year after the book was published in Greek, life changed. The collapse of the Greek and European economies pushed me through the rabbit hole of a ministerial position in the midst of an almighty clash between the people who elected me and a global oligarchy. Meanwhile, thanks to my new role, this little book was being translated into many languages, its musings acquiring a large audience in France, Germany, Spain and several other places. The only major language that it was not translated into was English.

Now, with the help of Jacob Moe, who translated from the original Greek, and the good people at Penguin Random House, Will Hammond in particular, it is appearing in the language in which I usually write. Following swiftly on the heels of another book, *Adults in the Room*, which was exceptionally painful to write, documenting as it did the traumatic events of 2015, reworking this book into its English incarnation has been therapeutic: an escape from the trials and tribulations of one caught up in the vortex of a collapsed and sinking economy. It has allowed me to return to a long-lost self who once wrote in peace and quiet, without the constant assaults of the press, doing what I have always loved: seeking ways to disagree with myself in order to discover what my true thoughts are.

The problem with our daily exchanges over the issues of the day is that we drift into a debate uninformed by the elephant in the room: capitalism. During the week in July 2017 that I worked on this English edition, again in Aegina, overlooking the same sea and the same mountains, I loved *not* writing about Brexit, Grexit, Trump, Greece, Europe's economic crisis but instead talking to my daughter, in the abstract, about capitalism. For, in the end, nothing makes sense if we do not come to terms with this beast that dominates our lives.

In view of what I've just written, readers may be surprised by the absence of any mention of 'capital' or 'capitalism' in the book. I chose to leave out such words not because there is anything wrong with them but because, loaded as they are with heavy baggage, they get in the way of illuminating the essence of things. So, instead of speaking about capitalism, I use the term 'market society'. Instead of 'capital' you will find more normal words like 'machinery' and 'produced means of production'. Why use jargon if we can avoid it?

Turning to my influences and sources, I have a confession: this book, courtesy of having been written as something of a stream of consciousness lasting a mere nine days, is riddled with ideas, phrases, theories, stories that I have been consciously or unconsciously collecting, borrowing, plundering since the early 1980s to shape my thinking and to help me come up with teaching devices that shake students and audiences out of lethargy. A complete list is impossible, but here are some that come to mind.

Besides the works of literature and the poems mentioned in the text, as well as the science-fiction movies without which I find it hard to understand the present, I shall mention four books: Jared Diamond's *Guns, Steel and Germs*, which underpins the story in the first chapter that explains the emergence of gross inequities and, ultimately, racist stereotyping; Richard Titmuss's *The Gift Relationship*, whose discussion of the blood market underscores ideas first developed in Karl Polanyi's *Great Transformation*; Robert Heilbroner's majestic *The Worldly Philosophers*; and novelist Margaret Atwood's *Payback*, which I recommend unreservedly as perhaps the best, and most entertaining, book ever written on debt.

Finally, it would be remiss not to mention the spectre of Karl Marx, the dramaturgy of the ancient Athenian tragedians, John Maynard Keynes's clinical dissection of the so-called 'fallacy of composition' and lastly the irony and insights of Bertolt Brecht. Their stories, theories and obsessions haunt every thought I ever had, including the ones laid down in this book.

1

Why So Much Inequality?

All babies are born naked, but soon after some are dressed in expensive clothes bought at the best boutiques while the majority wear rags. Once they've grown a little older, some get annoyed every time relatives and godparents bring them yet more clothes, since they would prefer other gifts, such as the latest iPhone, while others dream of the day when they might be able to head to school without holes in their shoes.

This is the kind of inequality that defines our world. From a young age you seemed aware of it, even though it was not part of your everyday life, because, truth be told, the school we send you to isn't attended by children condemned to lives of deprivation or violence – as the overwhelming majority of the world's children are. More recently you asked me, 'Why so much inequality, Dad? Is humanity that stupid?' My answer didn't satisfy you – or me, for that matter. So please let me give it another try, by posing a slightly different question this time.

Why didn't the Aborigines in Australia
invade England?

Living and growing up in Sydney as you do, your schoolteachers have spent many hours and lessons making you and your classmates aware of the hideous injustices perpetrated by 'white' Australia on the country's original inhabitants, the Aborigines; of their splendid culture, which white European colonialists trampled underfoot for over two centuries; and of the conditions of shocking poverty in which they still live as a result of those centuries of violence, theft and humiliation. But did you ever wonder why it was the British who invaded Australia, seizing the Aboriginals' land just like that, almost wiping them out in the process, and not the other way round? Why didn't Aboriginal warriors land in Dover, quickly advancing to London, murdering any Englishmen who dared resist, including their queen? I bet not one teacher at your school dared to raise that question.

But it's an important question, and if we don't answer it carefully, we risk thoughtlessly accepting either that the Europeans were ultimately smarter and more capable – which was certainly the view of the colonizers at the time – or that the Aboriginal Australians were better and nicer people, which is why they themselves didn't become brutal colonizers. Even if it were true, this second argument boils down to much the same thing as the first: it says there is just something intrinsically different between white Europeans and Aboriginal Australians, without explaining how or why, and nothing legitimizes crimes like those committed upon the Aborigines, and others, better than arguments of this sort.

These arguments must be silenced if only because they can emerge from within your own mind, tempting you to accept that history's victims deserved what they got because they were not smart enough.

So the original question, 'Why so much inequality between peoples?' blends into another, more sinister question: 'Is it not simply that some groups of people are smarter and, as a result, more capable than others?' If this is not the case, why is it you've never seen in the streets of Sydney the kind of poverty you encountered on your visit to Thailand?

Markets are one thing, economies another

In the bubble of Western prosperity you're growing up in most grown-ups would say to you that poor countries are poor because their 'economies' are weak – whatever that means. They would also say to you that poor people in your own community are poor because they do not have anything to sell that others really want – that, in short, they have nothing to offer the 'market'.

This is why I have decided to talk to you about something called the economy: in your world, and mine, any discussion of why some people are poor whereas others are stinking rich, or even why humanity is destroying Planet Earth, revolves around that thing called the economy. And the economy is related to that other thing known as the market. To have any say in humanity's future, you cannot afford to roll your eyes and switch off the moment words like 'economy' or 'market' are mentioned.

So, let me begin with a common error that many make: they think that markets and the economy are one and the same thing. They are not. What exactly are markets? Markets are places of exchange. At the supermarket we fill our trolley with things in exchange for money, which the seller – the owner of the supermarket or the employee paid with money from the register – later exchanges for other things that they want. Before money was invented, exchanges were direct: a banana would be exchanged directly for an apple, or maybe two apples. Today, with the Internet in full swing, a market does not even have to be a physical place, like when you get me to buy you apps on iTunes or vinyl records from Amazon.

Obviously, we've had markets since we were living up in the trees, since before we developed the capacity to grow food. The first time one of our ancestors offered to trade a banana for some other fruit, a market exchange of sorts was in the air. But this was not a true economy. For an economy to come into being, something else was needed: a capacity to go beyond just gathering bananas from trees or hunting animals – a capacity to produce food or instruments that would not have existed without human labour.

Two Big Leaps: speech and surplus

Some eighty-two thousand years ago humans made the First Big Leap: using our vocal chords we managed to speak and move beyond inarticulate cries. Seventy thousand years later (that is, twelve thousand years ago) we made the Second Big Leap: we succeeded in cultivating land. Our ability to speak and to produce food – instead of just shouting about and consuming what the environment naturally provided (wild game, nuts, berries, fish) – gave rise to what we now call the economy.

Today, twelve thousand years after humanity 'invented' agriculture, we have every reason to recognize that moment as truly historic. For the first time humans managed not to rely on nature's bounty; they learned, with great effort, to make it produce goods for their own use. But was this a moment of joy and exaltation? Not at all! The only reason humans learned to cultivate the earth was that they were starving. Once they had hunted down most of their prey with savvy hunting methods, and multiplied in number so rapidly that produce from the trees was insufficient, humans were forced by dire need to adopt methods for cultivating the land.

Like all technological revolutions, this wasn't one that humanity consciously decided to start. Where humans could avoid it, as in Australia where nature provided enough food, they did so. Farming took hold where humans would have perished otherwise. Gradually, through experimentation and observation, the technology that allowed us to farm more efficiently evolved. But in the process, as we developed the means to grow food, human society changed drastically. For the first time agricultural production created the basic element of a true economy: surplus.

What is surplus? Initially, surplus simply meant any produce of the land that was left over after we had fed ourselves and replaced the seeds used to grow it in the first place. In other words, surplus is the extra bit that allows for accumulation and future use – for example, wheat saved for a 'rainy day' (if the next harvest were to be destroyed by hail) or used as extra seeds to be planted next year, increasing production, and the surplus, in the years to come.

You should take note of two things here. First, hunting, fishing and the harvesting of naturally occurring fruit and vegetables could never yield a surplus even if the hunters, the fishermen and the gatherers were super-productive. Unlike grains – corn, rice and barley, which could be preserved well – fish, rabbits and bananas quickly rotted or spoiled. Second, the production of agricultural surplus gave birth to the following marvels that changed humanity for ever: writing, debt, money, states, bureaucracy, armies, clergy, technology and even the first form of biochemical war. Let's take these one by one ...

Writing

We know from archaeologists that the first forms of writing emerged in Mesopotamia, which is where Iraq and Syria are now. But what did they record? The quantity of grain that each farmer had deposited in a shared granary. This was only logical: it was difficult for each individual farmer to build a granary for storing their surplus, and simpler if there was a common granary overseen by a guard, which every farmer could use. But such a system required some sort of receipt, for example, that Mr Nabuk had deposited a hundred pounds of grain in the granary. Indeed, writing was first created so that these accounting records could be kept – so that each individual could prove what quantity they had stored in a common granary. It is no coincidence that societies not in need of developing agricultural cultivation – in places where wild game, nuts and berries were never in short supply, as was the case for Aboriginal Australian societies and indigenous communities in South America – kept to music and painting and never invented writing.

Debt, money and the state

Accounting records of how much wheat belonged to our friend Mr Nabuk were the very beginnings of both debt and money. Based on archaeological finds, we know that many workers were paid in shells engraved with numbers indicating the pounds of grain that rulers owed them for their labour in the fields. Since the amounts of grain these shells referred to had often not been harvested yet, the shells were a form of debt owed to workers by their rulers. At the same time, the shells were also a form of currency, since workers could exchange them for products produced by others.

But the most interesting discovery has to do with the first appearance of metal currency. Most people believe it was invented to be used in transactions, but this wasn't the case. In Mesopotamia at least metal currency that didn't physically exist was used in written accounts to express how much farm workers were owed. For example, the accounting log would note, 'Mr Nabuk has received grain valued at three metal coins,' even though those metal coins had not been minted yet and might not be for many, many years. In a sense, this imagined form of money, used to facilitate real exchanges, was a virtual currency. So, when people tell you that today's economy is very different to the economy of the past, citing the virtual payments made possible by digital technologies, tell them that is nothing new; that virtual money has existed ever since the economy was invented, following the agricultural revolution twelve thousand years ago and the creation of the first surplus.

In fact, even when metal currency was forged, it was often too heavy to circulate. So, the value of the grain Mr Nabuk was owed was expressed as a proportion of the weight of a large piece of iron. In any case, Mr Nabuk never went around with metal currency in his pocket – all he carried on him was an IOU, often in the form of a shell with writing on it indicating pounds of grain or shares of a large, immovable block of iron.

Now the thing about virtual currency and these IOUs is that to work they need a great deal of … faith. Mr Nabuk had to believe – he must have had *faith* – in the willingness and capacity of the controllers of the granary to give him the grain he was owed once it was produced. And others must have believed that too before accepting Mr Nabuk's shell-IOUs in exchange for oil or salt or in order to help him build his hut. This is the origin of the word 'credit': it comes from the Latin *credere*, which means 'to believe'.

For such faith to prevail and give value to the shells (i.e. the currency), people needed to know that they were guaranteed by someone or something very powerful. This might be a ruler descended from the gods, a mighty king of royal blood or, later, something resembling a state or a government: an authority that could be trusted to have the future power to reimburse Mr Nabuk with his share of the grain surplus, even if the individual ruler were to die.

Bureaucracy, army, clergy

Debt, money, faith and state all go hand in hand. Without debt there is no easy way to manage agricultural surplus. As debt appeared, money flourished. But for money to have value, an institution, the state, had to make it trustworthy. When we talk about the economy, this is what we are talking about: the complex relations that emerge in a society with a surplus.

And as we examine these relations, what also becomes clear is that a state could never have been born *without* surplus, since a state requires bureaucrats to manage public affairs, police to safeguard property rights and rulers who – for better or for worse – demand a high standard of living. None of the above would be conceivable without a hefty surplus to sustain all of these people without them having to work in the fields. Nor could an organized army exist without a surplus – and without an organized army the power of the ruler, and by extension the state, could not be imposed, and the society's surplus would be more vulnerable to external threats.

Bureaucracies and armies were made possible by agricultural surpluses, which in turn created the need for bureaucracies and armies. The same was true of the clergy. The clergy? Yes, surplus begat organized religion! Let's see why.

Historically, all the states resulting from agricultural societies distributed their surplus in an outrageously unequal manner, to the benefit of those with social, political and military power. But as strong as these rulers were, they were never strong enough to face down the vast majority of impoverished farmers, who if they joined forces could overthrow the exploitative regime in a matter of hours. So, how did these rulers manage to maintain their power, distributing surplus as they pleased, undisturbed by the majority?

The answer is: by cultivating an ideology which caused the majority to believe deep in their hearts that only their rulers had the right to rule. That they lived in the best of all possible worlds. That everything was the way it was destined to be. That the situation on the ground reflected some divine order. That any opposition to them clashed with that divine power's will, threatening to send the world spinning out of control.

Without this legitimizing ideology, the power of the state didn't stand a chance. Just as the state had to exist in perpetuity, surviving the death of its ruler, the ideological crutch for state power needed to be institutionalized too. The people who performed and instituted the ceremonies that served this purpose were the clergy.

Without a large surplus there would be no capacity to create religious institutions with complicated hierarchies of clergy, since the 'holy' men and women did not produce anything. At the same time, without organized religion the rulers' authority over the generation and distribution of the surplus would be very unstable and prone to insurrections by the majority, whose share of the surplus was usually tiny. This is why for thousands of years the state and the clergy were one and the same.

Technology and biochemical war

The human brain managed to bring about technological revolutions well before agricultural production came about – for example, the invention of fire, metal extraction from ore, the aerofoil, as in the Australian Aborigines' remarkable boomerang. But agricultural surplus gave technology a gigantic boost by simultaneously giving rise to new technological needs – the need for ploughs and irrigation systems – and by concentrating resources in the hands of a powerful few. The agricultural revolution catapulted human technology to a level that made possible the construction of the magnificent Pyramids, the Parthenon and the Inca temples – with the help, of course, of thousands of slaves.

But surplus also creates deadly bacteria and viruses. When tons of wheat are piled into common granaries, surrounded by throngs of people and animals in towns and cities that lack basic waste disposal systems, the result is a massive biochemical laboratory in which bacteria and viruses rapidly develop and proliferate and cross from one species to another. Human bodies had not evolved to cope with the resulting devastating diseases, and at first many died. But slowly, over generations, the inhabitants of these societies managed to adjust to cholera, typhus and the flu and became more resistant to them.

Of course, when they encountered tribes and communities that had not yet developed agricultural production, because of the millions of deadly micro-organisms they now carried with them a handshake was enough to wipe most of the tribespeople out. In fact, both in Australia and America many more of the native populations died from contact with bacteria and viruses carried by invading Europeans than from cannonballs, bullets and knives. In some cases the European raiders even engaged knowingly in biochemical war: on one occasion a Native American tribe was devastated when a delegation of European colonists gifted them blankets knowingly seeded with smallpox virus.

Back to the question: Why did the British invade Australia and not the opposite?

Time to revisit the tough question I started off with. Why did the British invade Australia instead of the Aborigines invading England? More generally, why did all imperialist superpowers emerge in Eurasia and not one from Africa or Australia? Does it have to do with DNA? Certainly not. The answer lies in what I have just been telling you.

We saw how *in the beginning ... was surplus*. And from agricultural surplus there emerged writing, debt, money and states – and from these economies emerged technologies and armies. Simply put, the geographical conditions in Eurasia – the nature of the land and the climate – meant that agriculture and surplus and all that went with it took hold with great force, leading to the emergence of rulers of states in command of armies equipped with technologies such as guns and made even more lethal by the biochemical weapons they carried in their bodies and on their breath.

In countries like Australia, however, things were different. For a start, food was never in short supply since three to four million people living in relative harmony with nature had exclusive access to the flora and fauna of a continent the size of Europe. As a result, there was no reason to invent the agricultural technology that allows for the accumulation of surplus or for that technology to be adopted when the opportunity presented itself.

Today we know – you at least certainly do – that the Aborigines had poetry, music and myths of tremendous cultural value, but they didn't have the means to attack other peoples or to defend themselves from the armies, the weapons and the germs that agricultural surplus-producing economies engender. In contrast the British, coming from Eurasia, had been forced by climate and need to generate large surpluses and all that came with them, from seagoing vessels to biochemical weapons. As a result, when they arrived on the Australian coast, the Aborigines didn't stand a chance.

'And what about Africa?' you might reasonably ask. 'Why did not a single African country grow powerful enough to threaten Europe? Why was the slave trade such a one-way street? Maybe the Africans weren't as capable as the Europeans after all?'

Nothing of the sort. Take a look at a map and compare Africa's shape to Eurasia's. The first thing you'll notice is that Africa extends more to the north and south than it does to the east and west, starting off at the Mediterranean, extending south to the equator and then continuing until it reaches the temperate climates of the southern hemisphere. Now take a glance at Eurasia. It does just the opposite, beginning on the Atlantic and spreading east all the way to the Chinese and Vietnamese coasts on the Pacific Ocean.

What does this mean? It means that if you crossed Eurasia from the Pacific to the Atlantic you'd encounter relatively few changes in climate, whereas in Africa, as you travel from Johannesburg in the south to Alexandria in the north, you would pass through all kinds of climatic zones – some, such as the tropical jungle or the Sahara Desert, very extreme. And why does this matter? Simply because African societies that developed agricultural economies (current-day Zimbabwe, for example) found it much harder to expand, since their crops didn't travel well, refusing to take root further north, by the equator – or even worse, in the Sahara. On the other hand, once the peoples of Eurasia discovered agricultural production, they expanded west or east almost at will. Their crops (wheat in particular) could be planted further and further afield, forming a single fairly homogenous farming realm from Lisbon to Shanghai. It was the perfect terrain on which to mount invasions – with one farming people hijacking another's surpluses and adopting their technologies – and to fashion entire empires.

Another type of inequality

Geographical conditions predetermined that Africa, Australia and the Americas would be colonized by Europeans. It had nothing to do with DNA, character or intelligence. To put it simply but accurately, it was all due to the shape and location of the different continents. But there's also another type of inequality that geography cannot explain: inequality within the same community or country. To understand this kind of inequality, we need to talk about the economy.

Remember how agricultural surplus gave rise to the state and clergy? Its accumulation both required and led to an over-concentration of power, and consequently wealth, among the few who ruled over the rest – known as the oligarchy, which comes from the Greek words *oligoi* ('the few') and *arkhein* ('to rule').

It is easy to see how this is a self-perpetuating process: those privileged to have access to accumulated surplus are rewarded with economic, political and even cultural power, which they can then use to acquire an even larger share of the surplus. Ask anyone with business experience and they will confirm that it is much easier to make a million pounds once you've already got several million. On the other hand, if you've got nothing even a thousand pounds might seem like an unreachable dream.

So, inequality flourishes at two levels: first on a global level, which explains why certain countries entered the twentieth and twenty-first centuries dirt poor, while others enjoyed all the advantages of power and wealth, often secured by looting the poorer countries. The other level is within societies themselves, although it's often the case that the few wealthy individuals in the poorest of countries are wealthier than many of the richest citizens of wealthier nations.

The story I've told you thus far traces the origins of both types of inequality back to the production of economic surplus during humanity's first technological revolution – the development of agriculture. In the next chapter let's continue the story of inequality with the next technological revolution, which brought us machines such as the steam engine and the computer as well as the society you are growing up in, complete with levels of inequality that farming alone was incapable of achieving.

But before that a word of encouragement.

Inequality as a self-perpetuating ideology

When I referred to the clergy and its role, I mentioned how ideology works to legitimize the unequal distribution of surplus in everyone's eyes – both the haves and have-nots. It works effectively to the degree that it creates a web of beliefs, something like a mythology.

If you think about it, nothing is reproduced with greater ease than the faith of the haves that they deserve what they get. Since childhood you have been caught up in a vicious logical contradiction that you barely noticed. On the one hand, you were appalled by the idea that some kids cry themselves to sleep because they are hungry. On the other, you were thoroughly convinced (like all children) that your toys, your clothes and your house were all rightfully yours. Our minds automatically equate 'I have X' with 'I deserve X'. When our eyes fall on those who lack the bare necessities, we immediately sympathize and express outrage that they do not have enough, but we do not for a moment allow ourselves to think that their deprivation may be the product of the same process that led to our affluence. This is the psychological mechanism that convinces the haves and those in power (who are usually the same people) that it is right, proper and necessary for them to have more while others have much less.

Don't be too hard on them. It's incredibly easy to convince ourselves that the order of things – especially

24

when it favours us – is logical, natural and just. But at the same time be hard on your own temptation to accept the inequalities that you, today, as a teenager, find outrageous. When you feel as if you're about to give in to the idea that outrageous inequality is somehow unavoidable, remember how it all begins: with babies born naked into a society that segregates those it will dress up in expensive outfits and the others, whom it condemns to hunger, exploitation and misery. Maintain your outrage but sensibly, tactically, so that when the time comes you can invest it in what needs to be done to make our world truly logical, natural and just.

2

The Birth of the Market Society

It's dusk on the island of Aegina. Summertime. We are sitting on our veranda, gazing across the sea at the bright red sun as it sinks behind the Peloponnese Mountains. Just as my dad used to do to me when I was young, I turn to you and start explaining in scientific terms why the sun appears red as it disappears behind the horizon. Your moment is ruined.

Later that same evening we take our boat with our friends and their young son Paris to our usual taverna on Marathonas Beach. As we are ordering dinner, Paris starts joking about – he's on a roll and eventually we're all cracking up, even you, who are always last to laugh in case you seem less cool than you are.

Before the food arrives, Captain Kostas, who has tied up his fishing boat next to ours at the quay opposite the taverna, asks a favour of you. His anchor is stuck under a rock on the seabed, and the chain has snapped from his attempts at pulling it out. 'Please,' he asks, 'since I know how much you like diving, could you jump in and thread this rope through the anchor chain? I'd do it myself but my rheumatism has been acting up today.' 'Sure,' you respond, seizing the opportunity to be the heroine of the moment as you proudly dive into the sea.

The sunset. Your annoyance at me. Paris's jokes. The joy of diving into the sea just because Captain Kostas asked you to. This is the stuff of your summer's joy. By definition, they are 'goods' – the opposite of 'bads' such as the feeling you get when a friend is hurt, when you have to do boring homework, when you feel lonely or uncertain about life. Now notice the great difference between these goods, which fill life with a deeply satisfying happiness, and the goods referred to in economics – the stuff that you find on the shelves of shops, that are sold on Amazon, that the TV keeps insisting you need. These are something more, perhaps also something less, but certainly something quite different. Although we refer to them as goods as well, another word for them, and perhaps a less confusing one, is commodities.

So, what's the difference between a good and a commodity?

Two kinds of values

Twilight on Aegina, Paris's gags and the dive you took for Captain Kostas – these things were never intended to go on sale. Commodities, on the other hand, are goods produced in order to be sold.

I don't know if you've noticed, but in the societies we live in we tend to confuse goods with commodities.

28

We tend to think that the more expensive a good is the better it must be. And, even more importantly, there is a presumption that the more money you are offered for something you can do or pass on, the more readily you will deliver it. But it's not quite like that. Yes, it's true for commodities: the higher the price we're willing to pay Apple for an iPad, or to our local taverna for its excellent mousaka, the more iPads Apple is willing to produce and the larger the quantities of mousaka the taverna's cook will bake. But the same thing doesn't necessarily hold true for Paris's jokes. If we told Paris that we'd pay him to tell more jokes, and in proportion to how much he makes us laugh, he will most likely think it weird and become self-conscious. The prospect of payment could easily make him lose his sense of humour. Or, let's take the example of you and Captain Kostas: if he offered you money to dive, you might not take such joy from it. Suddenly the value of a gesture made out of a sense of altruism and adventure would be lost, and it's quite possible that the small amount of money on offer would fail to make up for it.

True, if Paris becomes a professional comedian when he grows up, or if you become a professional diver, then his jokes and your dives will *become* commodities: you'll sell them for specific amounts of money – they will have acquired a *market price* – and this price will reflect their *exchange value* – what they are worth in a market in exchange for something else. But unless and until this happens, then their value is of a completely different kind. We might call it their *experiential value*. A dive, a sunset, a joke: all three can have an enormous amount of experiential value and no exchange value whatsoever.

These two types of values, experiential and exchange, couldn't be more different from one another. Yet very often in today's societies, just as all goods are thought of as commodities, so all values are measured – by economists, at any rate – as if they were exchange values. Anything without a price, anything that can't be sold, tends to be considered worthless, whereas anything with a price, it is thought, will be desirable.

One very good example of this confusion is the blood market. In many countries donors voluntarily give blood free of charge because they feel compelled to help fellow citizens whose lives are at risk. In other countries donors are compensated for the blood they give with money. Where do you think more blood is given?

Before I've even finished asking the question, I bet you've already guessed the answer: it has been observed that in countries where blood donors are paid for the blood they donate, the quantity collected is significantly smaller than it is in countries where blood is donated voluntarily, without payment. It seems that payment discourages more donors who want to give their blood free of charge than it attracts donors who care for the money.

Those who confuse goods with commodities fail to understand why blood donations decrease when donors are paid. They are baffled by the fact that potential blood donors decide *not* to give blood *just because* they've been offered money in return. But what's happening here is easy to understand if you recall the dive Captain Kostas asked of you. When he resorted to pleading with you to take a dive into the sea, at night, no less, so you could help him with his anchor, that sense of being a good, heroic kid made you overcome your fear of the dark sea and the inconvenience of undressing and getting all cold and wet and salty. It's very possible you wouldn't have done it if he'd said, 'I'll give you five euros to jump in the water.'

The same holds true in the case of donating blood. Many blood donors take pleasure from the idea of giving blood, but when they are offered a monetary sum for it, the shift from contribution to transaction ruins the pleasure, while the sum being offered isn't enough to make up for it, let alone the time and pain of having a needle stuck into one's arm.

Oscar Wilde wrote that a cynical person is someone who knows the price of everything but the value of nothing. Our societies tend to make us all cynics. And no one is more cynical than the economist who sees exchange value as the only value, trivializing experiential value as unnecessary in a society where everything is judged according to the criteria of the market. But how exactly did exchange value manage this triumph over experiential value?

The commodification of everything

Imagine the scene: it's Easter Sunday. We've been eating and drinking since morning. We grown-ups have been working two whole days, preparing the food, the house and the table. Early in the evening, after the feast is finished and the house is a mess, I ask you to help me tidy up the house a bit. You can't be bothered and ask, 'How much do you want, Dad, to let me off this chore? I'll get out my piggy bank and give you the money.' How do you think I would respond? Quite simply, no price would suffice to alleviate my disappointment.

In a family, among friends, in communities, people do things for one another. This too is a certain form of exchange, though not in the commercial sense, nothing like a market exchange. We're exchanging labour in the context of our own household when I wash up the dishes and in return you take the rubbish out. It is a type of exchange more like an exchange of gifts at Christmas or solidarity among neighbours who help each other when need arises. These exchanges are personal and reflect long-standing, deep, familial, communal bonds and feelings. In sharp contrast, market exchanges are exactly the opposite: fleeting, cold, impersonal, as in when you order a book from Amazon with the click of a button.

A long time ago most goods were produced outside the circuit of commercial transactions – in other words outside the market. They were produced in a manner closer to how we divide labour within our home. This of course does not necessarily mean that the world was a better, more ethical place. For centuries if not millennia, women were given the worst tasks within patriarchal, sexist households, not to mention the serfs and the slaves who did all the drudgery in real or virtual shackles. The very fact that most work, most production, took place within the confines of the extended household gave rise to the word *oikonomia*, which comprises two words: *oikos* ('household') and *nomoi* ('laws, rules, constraints'). This is the etymology of 'economy', which literally means something like the 'laws of running, or managing, a household'.

A farming family would produce its own bread, cheese, sweets, meat, clothes and so on. In good years, when the harvest was plentiful and there were crops to spare, surplus produce such as extra tomatoes or wheat was exchanged with products made by other farmers that they were unable to produce themselves, such as scythes or apricots. In lean years, when belts were tightened and deprivation occurred, these commercial transactions ceased, since there was no surplus to exchange for other stuff. For much of human history, a household economy mainly produced goods, but only occasionally produced commodities.

Over the past two or three hundred years, our societies have transitioned to a different phase of human history. More and more of our products have turned into commodities, while an increasingly smaller share of our productive efforts has ended up producing goods for personal consumption. If you take a look in our kitchen cabinets, for instance, you'll find plenty of stuff produced for its exchange value which our family could not have produced on its own by any means.

This commodification – and the unstoppable victory of exchange value over experiential value – doesn't end in our kitchens. Once upon a time farmers would produce their own raw materials, such as animal feed, fuel and seeds. These days they buy most of their raw materials from multinational companies that have the technological capability to produce feed that fattens cows faster and for less money, fuel capable of powering tractors made with the latest technology, and seeds that have been genetically engineered to make crops more resistant to heat, frost and even the chemical pesticides produced by those very same companies. In order to guarantee their profits, companies now use patents to assert legal ownership of the genetic material of seeds or even a new breed of animal they have engineered in the laboratory. In this way we've arrived at the point where the market has extended to such an extent that even genes can now have exchange value.

Little by little this commodification reaches everywhere: even a mother's womb gains exchange value when it is formally and legally rented by a couple that wouldn't otherwise be able to have children, so as to be allowed to implant in it their own test-tube-created embryo. Soon we'll be buying and selling asteroids in outer space, extending the empire of the market and the supremacy of exchange value from the microcosm to infinity.

In this process the word 'economy' has become a misnomer. In the society that you are growing up in it bears no relation to the original meaning of *oikonomia*. Most of what we produce and consume is created outside the *oikos*, the household. Thus, the laws of the household, the original economy, are now irrelevant and incapable of shedding useful light on what is going on in today's economy. Perhaps a better term for what is still called the economy would be 'agoranomy', as in the laws of the *agora* – the marketplace. But as economy is the word that everyone still uses, we will continue to use it too.

A world removed from the logic of markets

According to the ancient Greek poet Homer, as you know, the protagonists of the Trojan War toiled, quarrelled and even gave their lives in the quest to obtain 'goods' such as glory, the spoils of war, honour, the benefits of being in their king Agamemnon's good graces, and more. Homer tells us that the warrior Achilles, upset by Agamemnon's decision to claim some spoils which he himself felt he had won in battle, went on a long strike, wilfully refusing to participate in battles for most of the Trojan War. Even though Agamemnon knew very well that he desperately needed Achilles' help, he didn't think for a moment about proposing some sort of monetary incentive – offering him money in compensation for the spoils he had taken. If he had proposed such a thing, Achilles would have undoubtedly felt even more offended.

It wasn't just ancient Greek poets that equated non-commercial goods with true goods. Ovid, a Roman poet, recounted the clash between the Greek warriors Ajax and Odysseus over who would get the weapons of recently slain Achilles – exquisite artefacts, manufactured by the god Hephaestus himself at Achilles' mother's request. According to Ovid, the Greek generals agreed to hear both of their arguments before deciding who was worthy of wielding the fallen demigod's arms. Eventually, the arguments made by Odysseus, the ingenious architect of the Trojan horse, prevailed against those of the fearless warrior Ajax, who tragically took his own life after hearing of his peers' verdict.

How might such a dispute over valuable artefacts have been resolved today? Most likely we would have held an auction, after which whoever had paid the most money would get to saunter off with Achilles' weapons. So why didn't the ancient Greeks think of auctioning them? The answer is that an auction would have been pointless and offensive since what mattered to Ajax and to Odysseus was not the exchange value of the weapons. What mattered to them was a different kind of value altogether: the honour of being thought by their peers to *deserve* Achilles' arms. If ownership was decided according to who made the highest bid in an auction, then carrying off Achilles' weapons would be, if anything, a humiliation: every time the winner of the auction looked at his arms in their tent, they would be reminded of their failure to win them on merit.

The reason for this difference between their world and ours is the difference between a society with markets and today's *market society*. Back in Homer's day only a tiny minority of products passed through any kind of market. Commodities, markets and exchange value did exist and played an important role in antiquity: the ancient Phoenicians, Greeks, Egyptians, Chinese, Melanesians and countless other trading peoples travelled thousands of miles carrying all sorts of products from one end of the world to the other, taking advantage of variations in exchange value from place to place. But these societies weren't governed by the logic of the market. To understand how and why Homer's characters or people in the Roman empire or during the Middle Ages behaved, we would need to understand first and foremost their cultural or experiential values.

Just as the behaviour of Achilles, Odysseus and Ajax makes little sense to a Korean or American businessman today, so the behaviour of people today would be baffling to the warriors of antiquity. For, to understand why people around us behave the way they do, you must realize that their behaviour is embedded in market societies where exchange value rules supreme. Life in market societies can only be understood in economic (or rather agoranomic) terms. Of course culture, customs and faith are still important, yet even these remnants of a world in which the markets were marginal and experiential value still ruled tend to make themselves felt via their influence on markets. This is why I am going on and on talking to you about the economy.

The question now is: how and why did societies with markets become market societies?

The genesis of market societies

The process of production requires three basic elements:

- Raw materials that ultimately must be extracted from nature (for example, iron ore), tools and machines with which to work them, fences and buildings in which to house it all, a whole panoply of infrastructure – all this is known as the produced means of production, or as economists call them, *capital goods*.

38

- Land or space, such as a farm, a mine, a factory, a workshop or an office, where this production takes place.
- Labour to breathe life into the product.

In earlier societies none of these factors of production were commodities. They were goods but not commodities. Take human labour, for example. People always worked, perhaps even harder in the past than today. Labour, human toil, was everywhere, but what we now refer to as the labour market (think of the back pages of a newspaper in which employers post job offers) was unknown – unthinkable even. In times of slavery or feudalism the slaves and the serfs worked hard but did not sell (or rent) their labour to their masters. Masters simply took a large percentage of their harvest by force, often backed by the threat of violence. As for their tools (the produced means of production), they were either manufactured by the serfs themselves or by craftsmen who worked on the same fief, fed by the serfs in exchange for the tools they crafted – more or less like what happens at the family dinner table, where everyone contributes something. Finally, land wasn't a commodity either: you were either born a landowner, in which case you wouldn't even think of selling your ancestors' acres as doing so was considered an abomination, or born a serf and as a result destined to *never* own land yourself.

Market societies came about when most productive activity began to be channelled through markets, and these three factors of production were thereby transformed into commodities, acquiring exchange value in the process. Workers were set 'free' to offer their labour for money in newly formed 'labour markets'. Tools began predominantly to be made and sold by specialist craftsmen. And of course land finally took on exchange value as a result of being bought, sold and rented in new-fangled real-estate markets.

So how did this Great Transformation happen? Why, all of a sudden, did the three factors of production turn into commodities?

Global trade

As you can imagine it's a long story, and if I try and tell it in detail there is no chance that you will hear me out. So, in broad strokes, here is the general picture. Things got going with the development of shipbuilding in Europe, with the use of the compass (first discovered by the Chinese) and with general improvements in methods of navigating the seas. All this helped European seafarers discover new sea routes, which in turn triggered global trade.

Merchants from England, Holland, Spain and Portugal loaded ships up with wool from England and Scotland, exchanging it in Shanghai for Chinese silk, which was then exchanged for Japanese swords in Yokohama before the ships swung back westward, stopping in Bombay to trade swords for spices, which they then brought back to England to exchange them for *much, much more* wool than they had started out with. Then they did it all over again.

In the process products such as wool, spices, silk and steel swords became goods with international value – global products whose exchange value was determined internationally – and merchants or producers selling such goods in the new markets got seriously wealthy. Landowners in places like England and Scotland were appalled as they saw their social inferiors, merchants and opportunistic sailors, amass fortunes that threatened to dwarf their own, and at some point they began thinking the unthinkable: *If we can't beat the filthy merchants, why not join them?* As they looked out of the windows of their castle towers, and down upon the serfs toiling on their land, they wondered: *What's the use of these serfs planting onions and beetroots? What value do beetroots have on the international market? None!*

And so they made a bold decision: get rid of all those perishable crops, like beetroots and onions, that offer no access to the emerging global markets; build fences around their estates, creating in this manner large enclosures; evict the swarms of pathetic serfs and replace them with flocks of sheep, which were more submissive and whose wool could be sold for a mint internationally. Thus, Britain experienced one of the most violent transformations in human history, the so-called *enclosures*.

Within a few decades nothing would be the same again. The British countryside completely changed in appearance. The sense of continuity that had prevailed for centuries among the serfs – who had lived for generation after generation on the same land, with the same lords, taking after their parents' habits and occupations – was abruptly ended. More than 70 per cent of the peasants were thrown out of their houses and off their ancestral lands. It was devastating, brutal, cruel and … highly effective.

So began the process of Britain's transformation from a society with markets into a market society, because kicking the serfs out turned both labour and land into commodities. How? Well, what would you or I do if, all of a sudden, we found ourselves left out on a muddy road without a home in rural England? We'd probably walk to the next village, knock on the first door we came to and plead, 'We'll do anything for a piece of bread and some shelter.' There you have it: the birth of the labour market – a market in which humans lacking access to land or tools must survive by auctioning off their labour, by commodifying their toil.

And that's just how it happened. Former serfs wandered the rutted roads by the thousands, offering the only good they had at their disposal, their own labour. Unlike their parents and grandparents, who had worked without ever *selling* their labour, these former serfs were forced to become labour merchants – traders of their own labour. Tragically for them, the new labour market they were trying to create took many decades to get going properly. At first thousands of former serfs were offering their labour to very few buyers. It was only when the first factories were established, decades later, that demand for their labour picked up. Until then there weren't enough employers to absorb the legions of unemployed former serfs, so famine, disease and nationwide misery previously unheard of in times of peace struck.

The same thing happened with land. Once they had replaced serfs with sheep, landowners realized that an alternative to overseeing the production of wool themselves was to rent their land out to someone else at a price determined by the international market value of the wool it was capable of producing. The denser a pasture's grass, the more sheep it could provide for, the more wool it could produce and the higher the rent they could charge per acre. In short, once wool had an international price, all it took for the green and pleasant land of Britain to acquire one too was the eviction of the peasants and their replacement with nice fat sheep.

But who would rent the land and raise the sheep? Some of the former serfs would. It was either that or abject poverty. So they signed leases with the local lord in the hope that when they sold their wool on the market, they would make enough money for the rent and the pitiful wages they were paying the other serfs who worked for them, and have something left over to feed their own families.

Notice how all the serfs became merchants of some sort at the very moment their ancestral lands became a commodity. Previously, under the feudal system, the serfs had worked the land to feed themselves, and the lord who owned the land took his cut. The market was completely absent from the production and the distribution process. After the serfs were evicted, however, the majority of the population was forced to participate in some kind of market: most serfs participated in the labour market, where they struggled to sell the sweat off their backs and worried about the exchange value of their toil. A few of them continued working the lords' lands, though under completely different conditions: as renters whose rent was determined by the price of wool, and as entrepreneurs terrified of the fluctuations in the market value of that wool. While their mothers and fathers had lived with the fear that their master might not put aside a large enough share of the harvest to prevent them from starving when winter came, they now worried about something different: *Will we be able to sell our wool on the market for enough money both to pay our rent and to buy enough food to nourish our children?*

Factories: the grey laboratories of history

The enclosures brought together all the ingredients necessary for the soufflé known as industrial society to rise. But, as any chef will tell you, ingredients are not enough; heat was also needed. It was not until the second half of the eighteenth century that the requisite heat arrived. It came from grey, inhumane buildings, belching black smoke from their tall chimneys: factories, whose bowels housed the tireless steam engines conceived by the Scottish inventor James Watt. The Industrial Revolution had arrived.

'Why did the Industrial Revolution happen in Britain and not some other country, like France or China?' I hear you ask. Many reasons have been offered to explain this: some point to the fact that, as an island, Britain was at a geographical remove from the tumultuous wars that ravaged continental Europe, while the seafaring history this gave rise to conferred an advantage when it came to exploiting the markets for international trade. Others point to its wealth of natural resources, such as coal, its large population and its thriving overseas colonies, especially in the Caribbean, where slaves from Africa worked the lands of the British conquerors. But the most convincing argument I have come across points to three other factors: unlike other European or Chinese feudal lords, who commanded large private armies, British landowners lacked significant military power of their own, so enrichment through brute force rather than trade was less of an option. At the same time, British landowners benefited from a relatively strong central authority: a monarch in command of a powerful army, which came to the aid of these landlords when facing recalcitrant serfs resisting eviction. Finally, the fact that land ownership was relatively concentrated in Britain meant that the mass expulsion of serfs required the consent of a relatively small number of landowners.

To see *how* the Industrial Revolution took place in Britain, let's go back to the cooking metaphor and think of Britain as a large cauldron. First, mentally place in that cauldron all of the ingredients mentioned above (landowners' military weakness, strong central government and so on) and let them marinate for a bit. Next add the accumulating wealth of the merchant class and those members of the aristocracy who had profited from the global trade in certain commodities, including wool products, fabrics and metals. Then add hordes of unemployed former serfs begging on the streets for a piece of bread, for work, for anything at all. Finally add the heat from Mr Watt's steam engines, which can power a thousand looms simultaneously, and stir vigorously. With a little luck, the Industrial Revolution will rise out of your cauldron in the form of the first factories. And it was here, in these 'dark satanic mills', as William Blake called them, that the descendants of the wretched former serfs eventually found jobs as industrial workers, sweating away, for the first time in history, side by side with the new steam engines.

The Great Contradiction

The triumph of exchange values over experiential values changed the world both for the better and for the worse.

On the one hand, with the commodification of goods, land and labour came an end to the oppression, injustice and wretchedness of serfdom. A new concept of freedom was born, along with the possibility of abolishing slavery and the technological capability to produce enough goods for all.

On the other hand it prompted unprecedented new forms of misery, poverty and potential slavery. With the advent of market societies and the exclusion of serfs from arable land, these landless former cultivators became either industrial workers or farmers who paid rent to landowners. In both cases they were now free to the extent that they no longer could be forced to work against their will, but their freedom came with new chains. While the waged labourers were free to do as they pleased, they were now entirely at the mercy of the markets – free only as long as they managed to find employers for their labour or buyers for their wool. Without land, they were free to go wherever they wanted, but were also at risk of the absolute deprivation of homelessness.

Those who did manage to find jobs worked over fourteen hours a day in the suffocating factories of Manchester, in the Welsh and Yorkshire coal mines, in the shipyards on the river Clyde. Newspapers at the time reported ten-year-old children in England and Scotland who lived chained to steam engines day and night in order to extract as much work from them as possible. Pregnant women worked away in the Cornish tin mines, some of them forced to give birth unassisted in the shafts. Around the same time, in colonies such as Jamaica and what was to become the southern United States, production continued to rely on the labour of slaves abducted from their homes in Africa and sold for their exchange value.

Nothing like this had ever happened before in human history. It may be true that humankind was globalizing from very early on – after all, as you know, all humans trace their ancestry to Africa. But the type of globalization that spawned the Industrial Revolution and was reinforced by it gave rise to the Great Contradiction: the coexistence of unimaginable new wealth and unspeakable suffering. As a result, the inequalities brought about by the agricultural revolution, which we encountered in the previous chapter, increased spectacularly.

'Money makes the world go round!'

You've heard the expression quite often. Though it's an unbearably cynical and miserably pessimistic view of humanity, it may – unfortunately – be largely true. But even if money is the be-all and end-all of life these days, what I'm really trying to tell you here is that it wasn't always so.

Money may have always been an important tool that helped people achieve their goals, but it wasn't a goal *in and of itself* to the extent that it is today. Under the feudal system a landowner would have never thought of selling his castle, no matter how much money he was offered. He would have thought it immoral and disgraceful. If he had been forced to do so out of need, he would have considered himself a humiliated and despicable failure. Today there is hardly a castle, painting or yacht that won't be sold if the price is right. In the triumph of exchange values over experiential values, as societies with markets evolved into market societies, something else happened: money was transformed from being a means into an end.

It is now time to offer you a simpler, more succinct, explanation of how this came to be: humanity invented the profit motive. But wasn't the profit motive *always* part of human nature? No, it was not. Greed, yes. An irrepressible urge to amass power, gold, works of art, fashionable friends, land – absolutely. But profit is quite different to all that, and no, it was not an important driver of history until fairly recently.

And now let me try out on you an even more puzzling idea: the rise of profit as a major incentive for people to do things came hand in hand with a new role for debt.

3

The Marriage of Debt and Profit

'Hell is where I am.' This is the demon Mephistopheles'
answer when he appears suddenly before Doctor
Faustus, the protagonist of Christopher Marlowe's
famed play, and Faustus asks if he has been suddenly
transported to hell. 'Wherever I go, I'm still in it,'
Mephistopheles explains.

I know that you haven't yet read this dark tale of how
Faustus sold his soul to Mephistopheles. The reason
I have not introduced you to it before is not because of
its macabre and disturbing narrative. After all, the fairy
tales of the Brothers Grimm, which you have read, are
much worse when it comes to gore and unpleasantness.
No, the reason is that it is all about a concept that is truly
inappropriate for children: debt.

Here's what happens in Marlowe's tale: Mephistopheles approaches Doctor Faustus with a tempting
proposal. He'll offer him twenty-four years of absolute
power and limitless pleasure on the condition that
Faustus promises to surrender his soul to him afterwards.
Faustus thinks about it and decides that twenty-four
years of omnipotence and bliss are enough, and that
Mephistopheles can do as he pleases with his soul when

the time is up. So he agrees. Mephistopheles smiles and asks him to sign a *contract*, which Faustus signs not in ink but in his own blood.

People have always created debts. When one neighbour helps another out in a moment of need, the latter expresses his thanks, saying, 'I owe you one.' Without having to sign a contract, both of them recognize that in due course the good deed will be reciprocated, settling their moral debt. But this kind of solidarity is different from debt as we understand it today in two ways: first, because of the contract, and second, because of something called interest.

A contract turns an informal agreement such as 'Lend me a hand today, and I'll lend you a hand tomorrow' into a legal obligation with specific terms that take the form of exchange values, often but not always expressed in money. Within that contract, known as a loan agreement, it is most often the case that whoever receives the loan (the debtor) will eventually pay the person giving the loan (the creditor) something extra in addition to repayment of the loan itself, usually more money. This particular form of profit derived from the giving of loans is called interest. So, here is the difference: in the context of solidarity, the incentive to help someone is the experiential value that you receive from doing the right thing, the warm inner glow you feel when you offer to help, just like when you helped Captain Kostas with his stuck anchor. But in the case of a loan agreement, of a legal contract, your incentive is to earn some surplus exchange value in return: to profit from the payment of interest.

In Doctor Faustus' case, Mephistopheles was not interested in solidaristic exchanges. Sick and tired of dragging people who deserved damnation to hell against their will, the demon wanted to snare a far greater prize: a *good* person who freely chooses their eternal torment. He does so by *indebting* the good doctor in a free and fair agreement. As the clock marches second by second to midnight at the end of Faustus' twenty-four years of bliss, the doctor naturally sinks deeper and deeper into despair and regret at the contract he had signed, realizing the terrible 'interest' he must pay.

The story of Faustus and his debt to Mephistopheles is important because it reflected people's worries at a time when their societies were transforming from societies with markets into market societies. It is no coincidence that Marlowe wrote his play in the sixteenth century, back when exchange values first began, little by little, to prevail over experiential values. In a story that illustrates the relationship between free choice, a binding contract, debt and interest, the play reflects beautifully the emergence of the profit motive in early modern Europe and the anxiety it caused.

That's why I'm telling you that the story of Faustus and Mephistopheles is no fairy tale; it marks a painful moment in human history, the moment when debt and profit partnered up.

Let's see how this happened.

The Great Reversal

In the age of feudalism the production of a surplus – which, as we saw in Chapter 1, is a prerequisite for the existence of an economy of any sort – went specifically as follows:

PRODUCTION → DISTRIBUTION → DEBT–CREDIT

To explain: first serfs worked the land and produced goods (PRODUCTION). Then the feudal lord sent his sheriff to extract his share, forcibly, if necessary (DISTRIBUTION). Finally, after he'd enjoyed what he'd taken, the lord sold any goods that were left over for money, which allowed him to buy things, pay for services and issue loans (DEBT–CREDIT). But as soon as land and labour were commodified, the Great Reversal occurred: instead of the distribution of surplus coming after production, distribution began before production had even started. How was this possible?

Recall that in England the serfs had been kicked off the land and replaced by sheep. Former serfs then rented land from landowners and supervised the production of wool and crops that could be sold for profit, so that they could pay rent to the landowner and wages to the few labourers they hired. In other words, those former serfs organized the production process like small-scale entrepreneurs, renting plots from landowners and hiring the manual labour of other landless serfs.

But to set this process in motion, these new small-scale entrepreneurs needed some money to begin with – to pay wages, get seeds and of course pay their rent to the lord – before they had produced any goods. As the former peasant turned entrepreneur never had enough money to pay for all this before his wool crop was sold, he had to borrow. Who lent him the money? Very often it was the lord himself, or local loan sharks, who then charged him interest. At any rate, debt came first.

And since the amount of money paid to waged workers as wages, the amount of rent paid to the lord, the sums to be paid for raw materials and tools were all determined and agreed even before production had begun, the distribution of the entrepreneur's future revenues was largely decided in advance of their existence – in fact, the only person who did not know how much he would end up with, after everyone else got paid, was the entrepreneur himself. In brief, distribution now preceded production.

This is how the Great Reversal took place, turning debt into the primary factor and the essential lubricant of the production process. This is also how profit became *an end in itself* – for without it the new entrepreneurial class could not survive. Think about it. If the price of wool suddenly plummeted or some natural disaster reduced output, they would not only starve but end up with unpayable debts. As the expiry of their loan agreement approached, they would sink deeper and deeper into despair. Unable to repay the loans and interest they owed, they would end up slaves to their debt obligations. Just like Doctor Faustus!

Wealth and competition

In the feudal system, as we have seen, serfs produced without supervision, simply keeping whatever remained after the landowner took his share. Wages had not been invented, profit-seeking was not a matter of survival, and debt was not a substantial issue for the majority. Consequently, wealth simply accumulated in landowners' grand houses and castles. Those in power amassed further wealth not through investment, commerce and profits but by looting other feudal lords or peoples, by conceiving plots that would bring them closer to the king's inner circle, by fighting foreign wars and so on. This was how they secured the power and glory they dreamed of. Profit didn't even exist as a concept in their minds.

However, with the arrival of business enterprises intent on making profits, a new source of wealth was created. Imagine water flowing from a tap into your bathtub. This is the money coming in to your business. Now imagine the bath plug has not been put in properly. The water flowing out is what you are spending to keep the business going. As long as the volume of water from the tap is greater than the volume of water draining out the plughole, the level of water in the tub will rise. The greater this difference between the water flowing in and the water flowing out, the greater the profit; the higher the water level rises in the tub, the more wealth is accumulated.

In the feudal system the dominant position of the aristocratic class was assured by their political, military, legal and customary advantages. Rarely was there any incentive to improve their technologies so as to increase productivity and increase the rate of wealth accumulation. In contrast, nothing and no one could or wanted to guarantee the emergent entrepreneurs their survival. Indeed, the prevailing political, legal and customary system was geared against them. This is why the only way they could ensure their survival was to profit. And because, unlike an aristocrat, anyone could become an entrepreneur – assuming they were willing and able to take on the necessary debt – every entrepreneur was immediately set against every other in a mortal competition for resources, clients and survival.

Whoever could sell at the lowest price would attract the most clients. Whoever paid their hired workers the least would stand to gain the most. And whoever could increase the productivity of their labour fastest would win both races at the same time. New technology could confer competitive advantage, and entrepreneurs had every incentive to take it up. This is more or less how inventions like James Watt's steam engine, which transformed workshops into factories, first came to be used.

Of course, the technology came at a price. To buy it, very often more money had to be borrowed. With additional debt came greater potential for profit but also a faster route to ruin should things go wrong. As the entrepreneurs' debts, profits and angst grew and grew, the competition between them became fiercer and fiercer. They *had* to pay their workers as little as possible, lest they end up bankrupt. Incredible new wealth thus grew side by side with burgeoning debt and deepening poverty. While the rich got richer, the bankrupt were ushered into the hell of the workhouse, and masses of workers faced ever harsher working conditions.

Do you see now how debt, not coal, was the real fuel that powered the engine of the Industrial Revolution, generating mountains of wealth for a few and unspeakable misery for the rest? In market societies all wealth is nourished by debt and all of the unimaginable riches created over the past three centuries ultimately owe their existence to debt.

Debt, as Doctor Faustus shows us, is to market societies what hell is to Christianity: unpleasant yet indispensable.

Doctor Faustus vs Ebenezer Scrooge

Returning to Faustus, you should know that the version of the story which most people read these days – and the one most performed in theatres – isn't Marlowe's play *The Tragical History of Doctor Faustus* but *Faust*, a much later version written by the German poet Goethe. While Marlowe wrote his play at the very end of the sixteenth century, Goethe wrote *Faust* at the dawn of the nineteenth. The basic difference in the two versions of the story is fascinating – at least from the perspective of the economy.

One difference is that in Marlowe's version Doctor Faustus conjures up Mephistopheles because he feels unconvinced by God and the scriptures. His is a religious, a philosophical rebellion. In contrast, Goethe's Faust is motivated by something baser: a crass desire for personal power for its own sake. The second and more important difference concerns the ending. In Marlowe's version, as I told you, once his twenty-four years are up, Doctor Faustus begs, cries and pleads to be released from his contract with Mephistopheles, but to no avail. At the stroke of midnight repulsive apparitions appear, who amid thunder and lightning carry him off to hell. Goethe, on the other hand, spares Faust this fate.

Instead of sending his hero to hell, Goethe allows him to achieve *redemption* through good deeds and wholesome intentions. Realizing his mistake before his time is up, Faust performs acts of public service and so, when Mephistopheles arrives to claim his *interest*, God's angels intervene. Singing, 'He who strives on and lives to strive / Can earn redemption still,' they take Faust to heaven instead.

Allow me to suggest one explanation of these differences. Do you know what today's money brokers – financiers and bankers and the like – call the repayment of a debt, including interest? They call it *redemption* as well. Is this a coincidence? Not in the slightest. The question of debt has been a religious one for a long time. Perhaps you've heard that Islam prohibits the collection of interest to this day, at least formally. Exactly the same held true for Christianity when Marlowe was penning his play. Like some Muslims today, Christians back then considered collecting interest on debt a sin, which they called usury. This is why the audience watching Marlowe's play, convinced that redemptions of interest-bearing loans were sinful, absolutely *demanded* that Doctor Faustus be punished, since he hadn't hesitated to offer Mephistopheles the ultimate form of interest:

the surrendering of his soul. But by the time Goethe was writing, things had changed.

And they had changed because, as we have seen, the transition from societies with markets to market societies that had taken place between Marlowe's era and Goethe's relied largely on debt and interest. The Industrial Revolution would simply not have happened without the suspension of the dogmatic rejection, and legal prohibition, of charging interest on debt. The stigma attached to the charging of interest was simply incompatible with the commodification of land and labour and with the Great Reversal. It had to be overturned – and so it was.

The Protestants, who broke away from the Catholic Church in the sixteenth century, played a crucial role in this reversal. Protestantism emerged in opposition to the Pope and the cardinals' monopoly of God. Protestants insisted that anyone could speak personally with the divinity, unmediated by an authoritarian, stifling Church. Suddenly, the person, the individual who is the director of his own affairs, became the pillar of that reformed Church. And who was the ideal example of this newly empowered, autonomous person? In an era when exchange value and the profit motive were triumphing, Protestantism's iconic hero was none other than the merchant, the entrepreneur. Unsurprisingly, the new Protestant ethic embraced interest-bearing loans and profiteering as part of God's plan.

The fact that Protestants and Catholics engaged in over a hundred years of war demonstrates what a violent societal shift this was. Thus, by the time Goethe's audiences were being edified by performances of his *Faust*, Europeans were far more forgiving to the indebted, as long as they paid up the original sum plus the interest due.

In a sense, Goethe's story of Faust was the inverse of Charles Dickens's story of Ebenezer Scrooge in *A Christmas Carol*. In Dickens's famous morality tale the penny-pinching Scrooge accumulates and saves wealth for his entire life, collecting mountains of interest but spending only the bare minimum. At the end of the story, when the Ghost of Christmas Yet to Come shows him his own death, how no one mourns for him and how a poor couple indebted to him rejoice at his demise, he sees the light, opens his coffers and begins to spend, spend, spend, enjoying his life for the first time by spreading happiness to everyone around him. If you think about it, Faust does the exact opposite. Rather than accumulating interest and rejecting the pleasures of life, he enjoys life to its full for twenty-four years, agreeing to pay a sizeable amount of interest in return.

Which of the two, Scrooge or Faust, do you think was more in step with the needs of the new market society that had come about by the time Goethe was writing? Faust, of course. Why? Because if we were all

Scrooges – misers who saved all our wealth without borrowing or spending – then the economy of market societies would come to a complete standstill.

It is to this phenomenon that we shall now turn.

4

The Black Magic of Banking

Like any ecosystem, a modern economy cannot survive without recycling. Just as animals and plants are continually recycling the oxygen and carbon dioxide that the other provides, so too must workers recycle their wages by spending them in shops and businesses recycle their revenues by spending them on salaries if both are to survive. And just as in our ecosystems, in which a failure of recycling leads to desertification, so when recycling breaks down in the economy we end up with a crisis that results in devastating poverty and deprivation.

As I am writing these lines, Greece, my country and the country that you consider your own even though you live in Australia, is experiencing such a devastation. Australia, the United States, Britain and most of Europe experienced a similar catastrophe back in the 1930s. It was so atrocious that it inspired John Steinbeck, an American author, to write a famous novel entitled *The Grapes of Wrath*. In the novel's twenty-fifth chapter Steinbeck tells the story of how, while millions were hungry, tons of potatoes were thrown into a river and crates of oranges were sprayed with kerosene in order to make them inedible. Instead of recycling, there was wanton destruction. It is at this point in the book that the author famously laments that, despite our ability to bring food from the earth, we are incapable of creating a system in which the hungry can be fed. This failure 'hangs over the State like a great sorrow', Steinbeck writes, while the anger of those who lack food grows like grapes on the vine: 'In the souls of the people the grapes of wrath are filling and growing heavy, growing heavy for the vintage.'

How could any of this happen? The answer lies in the way that market societies can very suddenly lose their capacity to recycle. And at the heart of that recycling failure, you will, if you look closely, recognize a familiar figure: the banker.

What is it about bankers that makes so many people dislike them? One explanation is that the rest of us are simply envious of their wealth. But, as I will now try to convince you, there is more than envy at work here. The deeper cause is that once usury was no longer considered a sin and bankers were allowed freely to charge interest on loans, banking began to acquire superpowers – the power to bring about vast amounts of recycling but also the power to bring recycling to a sudden and calamitous halt.

Allow me to explain.

Entrepreneurs as time travellers

Let's say an entrepreneurial wool farmer takes out a loan from a landowner in order to buy the commodities, labour, land and machinery needed to get the production process going and start a new business. What exactly is taking place here? In one obvious sense the entrepreneur is borrowing money from the landowner in the expectation that, when the wool he hopes to produce is finally sold, he will be able to repay the loan. Looked at in economic terms, though, you might say he is borrowing exchange value from the future and dragging it into the present.

If we had to portray this process in the format of a sci-fi movie, we would depict the wool farmer looking into the future through a semi-transparent membrane, dimly discerning on the other side what is to come. Seeing an opportunity, our entrepreneur now raises his hand, places his fingers on the membrane and then with a sudden jab pushes his hand through to the other side. He remains in the present, but his hand has crossed over into the future. Groping around, he grabs some exchange value and with another abrupt gesture pulls his hand back through the membrane to the present.

Assuming the entrepreneur has discerned the future sufficiently accurately, the sale of his wool harvest will be as successful as he predicted and will produce enough exchange value for the loan to be repaid. But if he is wrong and he fails to bring about the future in which that exchange value exists, then he will have disturbed the timeline. And as any sci-fi buff will tell you, this a big no-no. Unable to repay his loan, his business will fail.

If entrepreneurs are time-travelling opportunists, bankers are their incorrigible travel agents. In our sci-fi context unbounded entrepreneurial ambition translates into boundless future exchange value being snatched from the future and brought into the present via the time membrane. And while it is possible to borrow small sums from family, friends and collaborators, securing endless large loans is not easy. This is where the bankers come in.

Bankers as time travel agents

What do bankers do? Most people believe that bankers act as intermediaries between people with savings who have no immediate use for their cash and people without savings who want or need to borrow money. That they take deposits from savers, lend them to borrowers, pay less interest to savers than they charge borrowers, and profit from the difference. While this is how banking began a long time ago, it is certainly not what keeps bankers busy today.

Let's say that Miriam makes bicycles and asks a banker for a five-year loan of £500,000 so she can buy a machine that will allow her to build bicycle frames from carbon fibre, making them lighter and stronger. Question: where will the banker find the £500,000 pounds to lend her? Don't rush to answer 'From the money other customers have deposited in the bank.' The right answer is 'From nowhere – out of thin air!'

How? Simple. The banker just types a five followed by five zeroes next to Miriam's name and account number in the electronic database or ledger that lists customers' balances. When Miriam checks her account balance, she is overjoyed to see 'Balance £500,000' flashing on the ATM screen and immediately wires the money to the machine manufacturer. Just like that, a sum of half a million pounds has been created as if out of thin air.

A brilliant economist once said that 'the process by which banks create money is so simple that the mind is repelled'. That's so. The bankers' magical power that allows them to create money at the stroke of a pen or a few buttons on a keyboard makes us shudder in horror. Understandably. The reason is that it is hard to believe that value can be born from nothing. But let's go back to the moment the banker created £500,000 with a wave of his wand from nowhere. In a sense, the banker arranged for the present Miriam – an entrepreneur with a plan to sell bicycles – to sit in front of the time membrane and reach through it to the Miriam who will exist five years from now – a wealthy businesswoman with a successful bicycle company – and snatch half a million pounds from her, bring it to the present, invest it in the bicycle business and thus allow the future Miriam to become that successful businesswoman. In exchange for becoming *liable* for those half a million pounds during the five-year period during which Miriam turns from aspiring entrepreneur into successful businesswoman, the banker charges her interest and other bank fees.

Since they are not constrained to lend existing exchange value, bankers have every reason to keep conjuring up loans in the same manner – by a few strokes on their keyboards – for the more people they lend to and the more money they create for the economy, the greater the profits they retain for themselves. Just as laboratory rats, having discovered that pulling a lever results in being given a pellet of food, end up pulling it incessantly, bankers lend and lend and lend.

The Crash

Once upon a time prudent bankers would only lend to Miriam and her ilk if they trusted her to invest her loan wisely and be able to repay it further down the line. In other words, bankers were keen to see that their practices did not disturb the timeline – that, by the time the future came, the various Miriams would have produced enough surplus value to put back what they had taken from it. But in the 1920s or thereabouts banking became unhinged.

Two things changed. One is that in the aftermath of the Industrial Revolution the economies of market societies grew enormously and the debt needed to fuel them rose massively as a result. The other was that bankers found ways to insulate themselves from the fallout if things went wrong. For example, once they had granted Miriam's loan, they would then chop it up into little pieces and sell it on to lots of others. In return for lending the bank £100 each, five thousand investors would each be given a share in Miriam's £500,000 loan. Why would anyone invest in one of these shares? Because the bank paid them higher interest than they would have received had they simply deposited that £100 in the bank (but lower, overall, than the amount of interest Miriam had agreed to pay). Thus, the banker recouped the £500,000 immediately and still stood to make a profit when Miriam repaid her loan. And if Miriam were to go bankrupt and renege on her debt obligations, it was the five thousand investors who would lose out.

I know what you are thinking: there must be a catch. Indeed there is. The more money the banker transfers to Miriam from the future, the greater his potential profits and the greater the banker's capacity to earn money from other investors. But the more the banker uses his powers – helping to move increasingly large amounts of value from the future into the present – the more likely it is that the banker will disturb the timeline.

Suppose Miriam's business is successful: she produces her bikes; the manufacturers of the machinery bought by Miriam hire new employees; those employees buy bicycles and other goods; the process of recycling continues and market society moves onwards. But the more stable everything seems, the greater the incentive bankers have to use their magical powers more often and more freely. And though they barely notice, eventually their spells cross into the realm of black magic: the point comes when the loans they have made are so vast that the economy cannot keep pace and the profits being made are no longer sufficient to repay them.

At this point the realization dawns that the future everyone has been banking on will never come to be. And when those large quantities of value borrowed from the future actually fail to materialize, the economy crashes.

Suppose that owing to the bank's enthusiastic lending Miriam has taken on a debt too large for her business to repay. Eventually finding herself unable to do so, she is forced to close her workshop. It turns out that, with the help of the bank, she has been defrauded by her earlier self. Suppose Miriam is not alone, and a whole raft of businesses close down and a whole host of workers now find themselves unemployed. As a result, the shops from which those workers used to buy goods suffer too. As more shops and businesses close, the banks find themselves stuck with more and more loans that entrepreneurs like Miriam can't repay.

A rumour starts to spread that the banks are in trouble. Worried at the thought of losing their savings, some people who have entrusted their money to the bank in return for modest interest payments demand to withdraw their money in cash. Hearing this, other savers follow, fearing the same. But the bank does not have enough cash to repay them all, as it has lent it out along with the loans it conjured up out of thin air. As word goes round that the bank has exhausted its supply of cash, a bank run takes place: long queues form of people demanding their money back, and the hapless bank manager is forced to pull down the shutters. All of a sudden, even people with large savings in the bank find themselves penniless.

Remember when I said that debt is indispensable for market societies? That there can be no profit without debt? And that without profit there is no surplus? Now allow me to add this: the very same process that generates profit and wealth generates financial crashes and crises.

After a crash comes the slump. Everyone owes everyone and no one can pay. Savers are told that their money has been lost, as the bank they deposited it in is bankrupt. Even those with money stashed away cut down, fearing an uncertain future. The recycling process on which the economy relies starts to go into reverse. More entrepreneurs like Miriam lose their customers, cancel orders of new machinery and have to lay off workers. The fired workers cannot buy goods from the entrepreneurs who are still in business, pushing surviving companies towards the brink. Offices and factories close. Soon large numbers of workers, who would love to work, are unemployable, as employers, who would love to employ them, fear that the goods that they would produce will find no buyers.

Meanwhile, families cannot repay the loans with which they bought their houses. The banks confiscate their houses to sell them in a desperate bid to retrieve some of the missing millions. But with so many houses on sale and so little money in people's pockets, rows and rows of sad houses remain empty and house prices collapse.

Widespread insolvency. Mass unemployment. Wrath. This is the nemesis that follows hot on the trail of the bankers' hubris. Its wretched vengeance falls indiscriminately and so affects the poor and the innocent above all.

Who can put an end to this dizzying doom spiral?

The (not so) new role of the state

Once the economy is caught up in this destructive vortex, only one thing can help: the state. Since the nineteenth century, when market societies experienced their first slumps, the state – under pressure from its more powerful citizens – has been forced to intervene. But how?

Invariably, the first thing the state has to do is intervene in the banking system itself. From the moment panic spreads, one bank collapsing after the other, the only way to halt the destruction is for the state to put an end to this chain reaction by lending money to the banks so that they can remain open. But where can the state find so much money in such a short time?

You may have heard of something called a central bank. Each country – or to be more accurate each currency – has one. Central banks have different names in different countries. In Britain it is called the Bank of England, in the United States it is known as the Federal Reserve, in Australia the Reserve Bank. In continental Europe it is known simply as the European Central Bank. Whatever its name, a central bank is something like a state-owned bank whose customers are all the other banks, and it is from this central bank that the money comes – in gargantuan quantities.

The question that I can see forming on your lips is: 'But where do the central banks get *their* money from?' And I am sure you can now anticipate the answer: 'From nowhere – from thin air!' Yes, that's right. Just as Miriam's banker conjured up numbers in her bank account, the central bank does the same, only this time it puts it in the account that Miriam's bank holds with the central bank. And just as the bank that lent to Miriam was effectively agreeing to be *liable* for her debt until the time when she became good for it, so the state, with its yet greater power to command confidence and trust, effectively declares that it will be liable for the bank's debt until it returns to health.

The difference is that when the central bank conjures up money out of nothing – borrowing exchange value from the future – its motivation has nothing to do with profit-making. Its purpose is to save the bankers from themselves and to prevent the economy from being devastated by their black magic. By acting as the lender of last resort to normal banks, an interesting relationship emerges: the central bank acquires some authority over them. In theory, the central bank can decide which banks to save and which to let fail, and so – again, in theory – central banks should be able to place restrictions on the bankers' practices in the hope of restraining their black magic. In reality, this has always been a game of cat and mouse, in which the banker mice possess infinite options for bypassing, and making a mockery of, the obstacles placed in their path by central bankers. However hard central bankers have tried to stop bankers from starting uncontrollable fires, the bankers have almost always got away with arson, forcing panicking central bank officials to create rivers of new money with which to extinguish the flames.

Realizing how little trust the weary public have in central banks' ability to constrain normal banks, and in order to settle their nerves and prevent bank runs, governments have had to go one step further: they have guaranteed the public's savings as well, promising to reimburse them if the bank where they deposited it goes bust. Naturally, the only way that the state's central bank can do this is to conjure that money from thin air as well.

'From thin air!' I know: however often I may have used this expression, you will continue to find it weird, puzzling, unsettling. Most people, if not everyone, feel the same, and many assume that this is a new phenomenon – that before the technology arose which allows bankers and governments simply to type extra numbers on their digital ledgers, money was something more real, more tangible, more honest. This is a badly mistaken view.

Remember Mr Nabuk, the Mesopotamian farm worker whose labour was paid for with shells? And that on those shells a bureaucrat working for the ruler had written numbers indicating how much grain Mr Nabuk was due to collect once the harvest was in? In truth, there is no great difference between these inscribed shells and the money issued by a central bank. Mesopotamian rulers could in principle write any number they chose on as many shells as it pleased them to give out, not unlike what a central bank can do. What mattered then and what matters now is simply that the numbers on those shells or the figures on those ledgers are believable, that the productivity of the land and the wealth and stability of the state make those promises of grain and currency trustworthy. It is in this sense that the role of the state is (not so) new.

What is, however, terribly modern and only true for market societies is the fact that private bankers and not just the authorities now have the same privilege of conjuring up money from thin air as well.

Bankers and the state: a toxic relationship

You may now be wondering, *If bankers know that the state will come to their rescue in their time of need, what incentive do they have to limit the loans they dish out during the good times? Wouldn't a better solution be for the state to rescue the banks – so that people's savings and the economy's payment system are preserved – but not to rescue the bankers themselves? Why not send them home penniless as a warning to any other banker who is tempted to do the same?*

Unfortunately, this obvious solution crashes on the shoals of harsh reality. More often than not, the politicians in charge of government are elected with the help of large contributions from those same bankers. Too often, the politicians need the bankers every bit as much as the bankers need them.

It is a similar situation with the officials of central banks. Courtesy of their magical superpowers, bankers can pay themselves salaries far in excess of those paid by the government or the central bank without explaining these to a suspicious public, as the government must do. Sadly, it is often the case that the very public servants whose job is to supervise the bankers go on to accept jobs with these same banks once they have retired from public service. Knowing the potential rewards that await them, it would take an heroic disposition for those officials to act truly tough in their dealings with the bankers under their supervision. Alas, heroes are, and have always been, in very short supply.

This toxic relationship between bankers and the state ensures that bankers have no reason to be cautious. Yes, after a crash they restrain their activities for a time. Like a driver fined for speeding, they may drive well below the limit for a while afterwards, but they soon find themselves speeding again. Soon after the state authorities have bailed them out and stability has returned, the bankers will be at it again, creating money as if there is no tomorrow.

To conclude this distressing story, we now come up against a fundamental paradox. The instability that bankers create in market societies can be reduced but it can never be entirely eradicated for the simple reason that the economy is fuelled by the thing they provide: debt. And so it is the case that the more successful the state is in begetting stability, the safer the conditions are for creating more debt, the more exuberant the bankers are allowed to become – and the greater the instability they cause.

Unpayable debts

When a borrower goes bankrupt and is unable to repay their debts, what should be done? There can only be one solution: the debts have to be forgiven, or in economic terms *written off*. This isn't an ethical issue – whether it is right or wrong for one person to renege on debts to another – it's a practical issue.

In early Victorian times the law stipulated that those who could not repay their debts should be locked up in special debtors' prisons until they repaid them in full and with interest. Today certain countries are treated in the same way when their governments cannot repay their debts – our Greece being a case in point. But people forget that market societies survived the crashes and the slumps of the nineteenth century only because the law was changed to ensure that not all debts are sacred. Why was this done?

One reason is that when the bankruptcy of a company meant that its owners were incarcerated, losing everything including their homes, only very rich or very foolish entrepreneurs took on large projects carrying the risk of large unpayable debts. But for market societies to be able to build hugely expensive things like electricity stations and railways, and for corporations to grow beyond a certain size, the law had to be rewritten so that if a business went bankrupt it was only the property belonging to the business that was lost; the personal savings, home and belongings of the person who ran it were not confiscated. This is what came to be known as limited liability. (It is something of an irony that entrepreneurs who own companies should be allowed this protection from the bailiffs while little people who do not own companies are not.)

The more pertinent reason is that if a debt is never written off, then those businesses and families who are bankrupt will remain bankrupt for ever – not least because no one will lend to someone who is bankrupt. The unpayable debts hanging over them mean that they cannot ever hire workers, buy houses or send their children to university. If the business is a farm which produces fruit whose price has fallen and as a result its owners now face unpayable debts, they have every incentive to destroy much of their produce – even if others around them are starving – in a bid to create a shortage of fruit that will boost its price, just as Steinbeck described in *The Grapes of Wrath*. Similarly, if a government like Greece's today is held in permanent bankruptcy and forced to pretend that it can meet its debt repayments, it must extract taxes from businesses and families endlessly without ever recovering.

No company, no family, no country can recover if it remains for ever in the clutches of an unpayable debt. This is why in scripture it is stipulated that debts should be periodically culled, just as forests need some of their fallen branches to be burned in order to prevent devastating bush fires.

Naturally, those who are owed money – the creditors – kick and scream when they hear such words, and of all creditors it is the bankers who protest against the idea of debt relief the loudest. Bankers pull every string they can to convince politicians to legislate against debt forgiveness. And yet it is the banks above all who are responsible for the recklessness that makes such forgiveness essential, and it is the bankers who are least likely to lose their personal wealth or even the control of their businesses when the crash comes. If you need an example of double standards, look no further than this.

A world in which the bankers are rescued but all other debtors, including governments, are not: this is the worst of all possible worlds. In fact it is a sterile world in which the economy produces only instability, failure and the grapes of wrath.

But what can be done given the outrageous grip that bankers have over society and its politicians? The only salvation, once trapped in this manner, is for citizens to demand the coordinated intervention of the state to write off unpayable debts. This is the only way the atmosphere can be cleared of the haze of debt and the process of recovery can begin. Politics, in other words, is the only way to revive a faltering economy. It is also the only way that the root causes of its faltering can be addressed, but this is a matter for later.

The necessary parasite

As you grow up and experience more of the ups and downs of the economy, you will notice a piece of mind-bending hypocrisy: during the good times, bankers, entrepreneurs – rich people in general – tend to be against government. They criticize it as a 'brake on development', a 'parasite' feeding off the private sector through taxation, as an 'enemy of freedom and entrepreneurship'. The cleverer among them even go so far as to deny that government has any moral right, or duty, to serve society, by claiming that 'there is no such thing as society – there are just individuals and families', or 'society is not well defined enough for the state to be able to serve it'. And yet, when a crash occurs brought on by their actions, those who have delivered the fieriest of speeches vehemently opposing substantial government intervention in the economy suddenly demand the state's aid. 'Where is the government when we need it?' they yelp.

This is not a new contradiction. It reflects the problematic relationship the powerful have always had with the state. While they fear the state will intervene to curb their self-enrichment, they also sorely need it. The inequality that market societies generate – gigantic concentrations of wealth alongside widespread deprivation and poverty – makes them jittery. What other than a mighty state can protect them when the grapes of wrath have grown too heavy for the vines and the desperate masses congregate threateningly outside their fenced villas? But, then again, if the state has sufficient power to keep the riff-raff at bay, it will also have enough power to confiscate *their* property and throw *them* onto the street if the government were to fall into the hands of those thronging crowds.

One of the most prevalent arguments they make against the state is that wealth is produced individually, by heroic individuals. Taxation is therefore seen as an unjustifiable confiscation of what is rightfully theirs. Nothing could be further from the truth. To see this, let's go back to the beginning of market societies for a moment – to the time when the serfs were being kicked off their ancestral lands.

How do you think the landowners managed to get rid of the serfs so efficiently? The answer is: with the help of the state. The king and his government lent the landowners a hand, sending their soldiers in to put down any rebellion by the peasants. And how do you think the new order, underpinning market society, was maintained? How were the majority living under conditions of abject dehumanization in the slums of Manchester, Birmingham and London kept under control when a few streets away the minority lived in the lap of luxury? To put it simply, private wealth was built and then maintained on the back of state-sponsored violence.

State-sponsored violence isn't the only thing governments have provided for the powerful since then. Whenever the state has used its revenues to pay for roads, tunnels and bridges over which goods can be transported, to maintain the hospitals and schools that deliver workers' health and education, to support the downtrodden and unemployed, to police the towns and cities or to organize in any way the peaceful and stable functioning of society – whenever it has done any of these things (and many more besides), the state has provided the conditions in which individuals, especially the most powerful ones, have been able to pursue their path to wealth. Seen from this angle, the state has always provided the rich with a magnificent insurance policy. And the rich have returned the favour by doing all they can to avoid paying their premiums.

In fact, it is not just the state that provides the conditions for wealth creation. If you think about it, all wealth has always been produced collectively – through recycling and through a gradual accumulation of knowledge. Workers need entrepreneurs to hire them, who need workers to buy their goods. Entrepreneurs need bankers to lend to them, who need entrepreneurs to pay interest. Bankers need governments to protect them, who need bankers to fuel the economy. Inventors cannibalize the inventions of others and plagiarize the ideas of scientists. The economy relies on everyone.

Public debt: the ghost in the machine

While consistently demanding that the state continue to provide the conditions in which their wealth can grow, every time the high and mighty have received the bill for the state's services from the tax office they have grunted, moaned, whinged and protested. And since the powerful have great influence over the state, this has led to a curious phenomenon: the taxes asked of them have always tended to be low in relation to the amount the state has actually spent, directly or indirectly, on their behalf. As for the workers, their wages have for most of history barely been sufficient to feed themselves and their children, so their taxes have never amounted to a sufficient sum either. So where has the additional money come from? The answer is: public debt. And who has provided the government with the requisite loans? The bankers, of course! And where have the bankers found the money? I hardly need tell you that they have conjured it from thin air, just as they did with Miriam's loan. You can start to see how paying low taxes works doubly in the bankers' favour.

Yet, watching television, listening to politicians worry themselves sick over the size of the national debt, making all sorts of promises to rein it in, you might be fooled into thinking that government debt – or public debt, as it is known – is an awful thing, something like the smallpox virus, in need of permanent eradication. The argument made by those who consider the state an obstacle to private business is that a government that spends beyond its means and can't balance its books is heading for disaster. Don't fall for that nonsense. While it is true that too much public debt can cause major headaches, too little is also a problem. Even Singapore, whose government is forced by law not to spend more than the money it receives in taxes, finds it essential to borrow money. Why? Because a market society's bankers need public debt as surely as fish need water to swim in. Without public debt, market societies can't work.

When the government borrows, say, £100 million from a banker for, say, a ten-year period, in return it provides the banker with a piece of paper, an IOU, by which it legally guarantees to repay the money in ten years' time as well as pay an additional yearly amount to the banker in interest – say, £5 million a year. This IOU is called a bond, implying that the government is now bound for ten years to whoever possesses this piece of paper. Given that the rich refuse to cough up the kind of taxes that would make government borrowing unnecessary, the state issues bonds and 'sells' them to banks and rich people in order to pay for the things that keep the whole show on the road: roads, hospitals, schools, police and so on. By spending this money on its various projects – buying supplies, paying salaries – the government directly boosts the whole recycling process of the economy from which everyone benefits, including the banks.

But this is far from being the only reason that government bonds are useful to bankers. The one thing that bankers hate most is cash: money sitting around in their vaults or on their spreadsheet not being lent in return for interest. But as has hopefully become clear by now, banks become precarious and vulnerable if even a few depositors want their money back all at once. At that point bankers need to have access to something that they can sell in a jiffy so as to pay demanding depositors. Government bonds are perfect for this. To the extent that everyone trusts the government will be true to its word, its bonds will always be in demand. Indeed, they are exceptional in this way – no other debt can be recycled quite as easily. This means that bankers love government bonds: not only is a bond a loan than earns a nice rate of interest very safely (so much so, in fact, that it can also be used as collateral for taking out further loans from other banks), it can also be used as a commodity – a piece of property exactly like a painting or a vintage car that can be sold immediately if the banker is in urgent need of cash. Bonds are, in bankers' parlance, 'the most liquid of assets'. As such, they lubricate the banking system to keep its cogs and wheels turning.

In fact, in bad times, when bankers pick up the phone to the government and demand that the state's central bank bails them out, it does so not just by creating new money, as we have already seen, but also by issuing even more bonds and using them to borrow more money from other bankers, often foreign ones, to pass on to the local bankers.

You can begin to see why public debt is something much, much more than ordinary debt. It is a manifestation of our market society's power relations, the necessary response to the refusal of the rich to pay their share. It is also a shock absorber that allows accident-prone bankers to avoid many of the major mishaps that would otherwise occur in its absence. It is like an elastic band holding everything together, capable of stretching during the bad times to prevent the system from breaking.

Since the first human looked up at the night sky and wondered why she felt overwhelmed by its enormity, we have felt certain that there is something deep inside us, something indeterminate that gives us our capacity for wonder, dread, hope. Philosophers and writers have referred to that something as the ghost in the machine, the intangible power that makes us who we are. Allow me to suggest that when you hear politicians, economists and commentators talk about public debt as if it is a curse, you remind yourself that it is a lot more than that. It is the ghost in the machinery of market societies that makes them function, however well or badly they do. And when the powerful or their spokespersons demonize the state, scoffing at government and public debt, remember that they need the state as badly as they need their kidneys and livers.

But there is more ...

The black magic of banking destabilizes market societies. It massively amplifies wealth creation during the good times and wealth destruction during the bad times, constantly skewing the distribution of power and money. But to be fair, bankers are just that: massive amplifiers. The root causes of market society's fundamental instability lie elsewhere, buried deeply in the weird nature of two peculiar commodities: human labour and money.

Let us now turn to these and place them under the revealing lens of an ancient myth.

5

Two Oedipal Markets

In 1989 my friend Wasily, newly graduated with a PhD in economics, was struggling to find a job and coming up with nothing. As each month passed, Wasily dropped the bar a little further, applying for increasingly lowly jobs. Still nothing. Eventually completely disillusioned, he wrote to me in Australia, to where I had recently moved from the UK, telling me, 'The worst thing that can happen to a person is to become so desperate that you decide to sell your soul to the devil only to discover that the devil isn't buying!'

That's exactly how the unemployed feel when, pressured by the Great Need, they resign themselves to working for peanuts only to find that no one wants to hire them. I hope and trust that you will never find yourself in this position, but you should know that millions of people do. I also hope that you won't be influenced by those who stubbornly deny that this happens. But to explain why they do, let me tell you a story involving Andreas, another friend.

Andreas was complaining to me that he couldn't sell his gorgeous summer house on the island of Patmos. I replied that I'd buy it – for ten euros! He laughed, appreciating my pedantic point that there is a big difference between not being able to sell something and not getting the price you want for it. However, it is this same point that underlies the conviction of certain people that there is no such thing as unemployment, only workers who refuse to sell their work at a low enough price.

Unemployment deniers

Nothing adds more insult to injury than blaming the victim for their victimhood. It is the favourite tactic of the bully and one that women have suffered for aeons. In fact it is the same thinking that we uncovered at the very start of this book: that the oppression of Australia's Aborigines was caused by their own inadequacies.

Unemployment deniers, as I call them, think like this: if an unemployed person's labour can produce *some* value, *any* value, for an employer, then that employer will be willing to pay *something* for it. Just as I was prepared to offer Andreas ten euros for his house on Patmos, some employer would be willing to hire Wasily for, say, fifty euros per month. If Wasily is not willing to work for fifty euros per month, this does not mean that he can't find paid work. It means that, like Andreas, Wasily has not found anyone willing to pay the price *he* demands. Is it not Andreas and Wasily's *choice* to hold out for higher prices or wages? If Wasily protests that he cannot afford enough food or a place to live on fifty euros a month, the unemployment deniers shrug their shoulders and point to the fact that there are places in Africa where people live for much, much less. Wasily simply needs to lower his expectations.

Setting aside the intolerable meanness of such arguments, they contain a serious flaw in practical, objective terms. To understand why, we need to differentiate between the cases of Andreas selling his house and Wasily selling his labour. In the case of Andreas and others like him who need to sell their houses, if they *all* dropped their prices *to the floor* they would all undoubtedly find buyers – eventually. But if Wasily and other jobless people were *all* to drop their wage demands and were prepared to work for pennies, there is every likelihood that the result would be even fewer jobs available.

To see why this is the case, we need another story, one dreamed up over two centuries ago by the French philosopher Jean-Jacques Rousseau.

The stag, the hares and the power of optimism

Imagine a group of hunters in a forest. Equipped only with nets, bows and arrows, they set out to catch a stag, hoping to feast on it together with their families. They spot the stag in a clearing and decide to encircle it quietly, trying not to scare it. Their plan is to surround the stag, entangle it in their nets and then kill it with their bows and arrows, which are far too weak to bring down such a lofty and powerful creature from a distance. The problem is that it will take a long time to encircle the stag without it noticing, and if dusk arrives without success, they and their families will go hungry. They also know that failure is guaranteed if even a single hunter proves to be a weak link in the circle.

Let us now also imagine that in the same forest there are quite a few hares bounding this way and that. The hunters can kill the hares with their arrows fairly easily, but a single hare won't feed a family for more than one meal, whereas a stag will feed the whole tribe for days, and if even one of the hunters turns his attention to hunting hares, the project of capturing the stag will be ruined.

This is the hunters' dilemma. They would love to catch the stag collectively, cook up the perfect dinner, sing songs, be merry, fall asleep full and content, and then repeat the story of their great feat for years to come. If each of them is certain that all the others will remain committed to the stag hunt, each will do his best and none will be distracted by some bouncing hare. But if just one of the hunters fears that even one of his companions might fumble, he will assume the stag will escape and turn to catching hares in order to avoid returning to the encampment empty-handed. In turn, the rest will follow, forcing the whole group to abandon the stag and do the same.

Note the most important points here:

- The hunters prefer to hunt the stag together rather than to hunt hares individually.
- Each will dedicate himself to the stag hunt if he is certain that the others will do the same.
- In the end, if they *believe* that they will hunt the stag in perfect unison, they will hunt the stag in perfect unison. Equally, if they do *not* believe it, they won't.

This is a lovely example of the power of optimism, but also of the demonic strength of pessimism. In the context of the stag hunt, both are self-fulfilling. And this is the essence of Rousseau's allegory: if a goal can only be achieved collectively, success depends not just on each individual pulling together but primarily on each individual *believing that every other individual will do so*.

Why labour isn't like houses, cars or tomatoes

Rousseau's story of the stag and the hares illustrates the critical difference between the labour market and other kinds of market and thus between the cases of Wasily and Andreas.

Let's start by noting that the main reason to buy Andreas's house is because it allows the person staying in it to enjoy great weekends and summers on the beautiful island of Patmos. The same is true of a shiny red Ferrari: to the extent that some enjoy driving it (or enjoy other people watching them drive it), it holds great attractions. Tomatoes too: provided they aren't rotten, tomatoes provide a tasty way to fill your stomach. In every case the exchange value of the house, the car, the tomatoes derives ultimately from its experiential value.

But what holds true for cars doesn't hold true for the services offered by a mechanic. And what holds true for tomatoes doesn't always obtain for the labour of the farmhand who cultivates them, nor does it hold true for my jobless friend Wasily. Because unlike the house in Patmos, the red Ferrari or the tomatoes, no one wants the labour of the mechanic, of the farmhand or of Wasily for its own sake.

Consider Maria, who owns a business that manufactures refrigerators and who might be interested in hiring Wasily. Clearly, her decision to hire him has nothing to do with any experiential value she expects to derive from having Wasily around at her factory. It is determined purely by a comparison of two exchange values: on the one hand, the increase in her revenues that she anticipates will result from the additional fridges that Wasily will help manufacture, and on the other hand the exchange value she will forfeit by paying Wasily a monthly salary as well as the various other expenses that come with having an extra employee.

Suppose she thinks that by hiring Wasily her plant will be able to produce five more fridges per month. Whether she hires him depends on whether she is confident that there are enough customers out there willing to buy those extra five fridges for a total sum that surpasses their additional cost to her from hiring Wasily. In other words, it all depends on her confidence that there are at least five people out there not just in need of a fridge but who have the means to pay a high enough amount for it.

If the various Marias who own businesses are all confident that market conditions will be good and that there will continue to be enough customers with money to spend, then each of them will hire the various Wasilys, who in turn will see their income grow, allowing them to buy refrigerators, bicycles or whatever it may be. In this manner the various Marias' optimistic expectations will be fulfilled. Equally, if the various Marias are glum and expect poor sales, they will refrain from hiring the various Wasilys; incomes will continue to stagnate; the market for fridges will remain stuck in the doldrums, and, guess what, Maria and her fellow entrepreneurs will find their pessimism was vindicated by reality.

Of course, Maria, being a businesswoman, knows all this better than anyone, but it certainly doesn't make her decision any easier. One night she tosses and turns in bed, consumed with anxiety over whether to hire Wasily and others like him and expand her refrigerator business. Unable to sleep, she switches on her laptop to check her email and the latest news. Her eye catches an intriguing headline: TRADE UNION BOSSES DECLARE READINESS TO SEE WAGES OF THEIR MEMBERS FALL BY 20 PER CENT IN ORDER TO BOOST JOBS. The adjacent editorial explains that the trade union's leadership seems to have been convinced by the arguments of the unemployment deniers that if wages fall far enough the jobless will find work. What do you think Maria's reaction would be?

Unemployment deniers have no doubt that Maria will rejoice and think, *Brilliant! Now that wages are 20 per cent lower, it makes perfect sense to hire Wasily and a bunch of others like him. I'll do so first thing tomorrow morning*, before falling blissfully asleep. And it is true that, all other things being equal, any employer would rejoice at the thought of paying lower wages. The trouble is that those dastardly other things just refuse to remain equal. And the main other thing that changes drastically when wages fall across the board is the capacity of customers to pay.

If Maria is like most smart businesswomen, she is more likely to think the following: *Oh! My! God! For trade unions to be considering a voluntary wage cut of 20 per cent, imagine how tough things must be getting out there. Much as I'd love to pay 20 per cent less in wages, now that all of those workers will be getting paid so much less, who will have enough money to buy my fridges?* And if Maria is an especially smart businesswoman, which it so happens she is, she might even think, *Even if I were still confident of there being enough people out there to buy my fridges, this piece of news is bound to shake the confidence of other entrepreneurs. And if they stop hiring, then there certainly will be fewer customers, so I had better do the same.* In short, Maria is highly unlikely to offer Wasily a job.

Just like Rousseau's hunters, entrepreneurs struggling to remain profitable in a market society are playthings of their collective expectations. When the group is optimistic, their optimism is self-fulfilling and self-perpetuating. And when it's pessimistic, their pessimism is also self-fulfilling and self-perpetuating. The fact that they know this to be the case only makes it all the more certain that it is – and just like Rousseau's hunters, they may end up chasing hares even though they would rather not.

This is why the unemployment deniers are wrong: because the labour market is based not just on the exchange value of labour but on people's optimism or pessimism about the economy as a whole, and so across-the-board wage cuts may well result in no new hirings or even lay-offs.

Labour and money: two devilishly different commodities

Major economic crises like the ones that broke in 1929 and 2008 have taught us that, in addition to the black magic of banking, market societies are plagued by two other demons. We have just had a brief glimpse of one of them, lurking in the labour market. Let us now look at the second, which is to be found in an equally peculiar marketplace: the money market.

'The money market? What's that? Who buys and sells money?' The answer is that nobody actually buys and sells money in the money market – unless you are talking about exchanging one currency for another, which is a separate matter. No, in the money market what they do is *lease* their money – just as in the labour market, in fact, where strictly speaking workers lease their time rather than sell themselves.

In the previous chapter we saw what happens when entrepreneurs like Miriam borrow money and how their debts fuel the economy. We also saw how the eagerness of bankers to issue loans can so easily send the economy over a cliff. And we also know why entrepreneurs need to borrow in the first place, for every new business needs debt to get going. What we did not discuss is what determines how much an entrepreneur like Miriam decides to borrow.

There are people who insist that money is a commodity like any other. By their logic, the answer is simple: how much Miriam borrows is determined by how much she needs and how much she can afford. In Miriam's case, she needs £500,000 to buy a machine to manufacture bicycle frames. Whether she can afford that £500,000 will be determined by the price of leasing the money: in other words, by the amount of interest the bank would charge her for the loan. It follows from this that, taking the money market as a whole, the lower the interest rate, the lower the price of money, the more that people like Miriam can borrow; the higher the interest rate, the higher its price, the less that will be borrowed overall. (It is for this reason that in times of crisis the central bank tries to reduce interest rates in order to make borrowing cheaper and help the Miriams of this world get their businesses up and running or back on their feet.)

Unfortunately, the people who think this way tend to be the same people I called unemployment deniers, for their reasoning is similarly flawed. Let us return to that night when Maria was tossing and turning in her bed, tortured by the dilemma of whether to hire Wasily or not. Now imagine that as she is looking at her laptop, unable to sleep, she comes across another newsflash: CENTRAL BANK SOON TO REDUCE INTEREST RATES SIGNIFICANTLY. How will Maria react? Will she think, *Great! Time to borrow more money so that I can hire more workers and produce more fridges!*? Or is she more likely to think, *For the central bank to be cutting interest rates so drastically, things must be looking terrible – forget it!*?

As you may have gathered, we are back to Rousseau's allegory of the stag hunt. In the middle of a slump, just as a blanket wage reduction may do nothing to boost employment but even have the opposite effect, so too can the announcement of an interest rate reduction be interpreted as an act of desperation, inspiring pessimism among entrepreneurs and scaring them away from the stag hunt in pursuit of hares instead.

I hope now you can see what I mean when I say that deep in the bowels of the two most fundamental markets of any market society – the money market and the labour market – demons work feverishly away, impeding the economy's recovery from its slump. But to make clear how tragic this is (and perhaps to annoy you a little, as I know how you feel about my inability to resist an old Greek tale), here is another story that will hopefully bring to mind the consequences of these demons for each individual.

The Oedipus complex of labour and money markets

You've heard of *Oedipus Rex*, Sophocles' famous play. It's based on the myth of Oedipus, who killed

Laius, the king of Thebes, without knowing that he was his father, and then married the king's wife – without knowing, of course, that she was his mother. What makes Sophocles' play truly fascinating for our purposes is the manner in which the playwright handles the story's central theme, the *power of prophecy*.

Let's begin at the beginning: Laius of Thebes learns that his wife Jocasta is pregnant and asks the oracle to predict what will become of their child. The oracle answers with a horrifying prophecy: Laius will be killed at the hands of the son born to him by Jocasta. Terrified, Laius orders Jocasta to kill the child as soon as she gives birth, but naturally she can't bring herself to kill her baby, so she hands him over to a servant ordering him to do what she cannot. But neither does the servant have the heart to kill a helpless infant, so he takes the baby boy to a mountaintop, leaving him there to die alone of hunger and exposure. Soon, however, a kind shepherd discovers the child, names him Oedipus and takes him to Corinth, where he is adopted by the childless king.

Years later, Oedipus, suspecting that the king of Corinth is not his biological father, asks the oracle to tell him more about his parents. The oracle does not answer him but responds instead with another prophecy, just as horrifying as the first: 'You will marry your mother!' Terrified, Oedipus decides to flee far from Corinth to avoid that fate. During his despondent journey he passes Thebes. There he encounters King Laius by chance at a crossroads, where they get into a fight over who has the right of way. In what must surely be literature's first case of road rage, Laius is killed by his son – and so the first prophecy is fulfilled.

Later, Oedipus saves Thebes from a monster called the Sphinx, lifting its curse on the city by solving the Sphinx's riddle. According to a third prophecy, whoever did so would become the city-state's monarch, and so Oedipus is crowned king of Thebes and, as custom ordains, marries the late king's widow, Jocasta, his mother – thus fulfilling the second prophecy.

What does this myth have to do with labour and money markets? Everything, for it demonstrates how terribly self-fulfilling prophecies can be. After all, if the first prophecy hadn't been uttered, King Laius would never have given instructions for his son Oedipus to be killed, the boy would have grown up in the palace of Thebes and, knowing who his true father was, would never have killed him. The same is true of the second prophecy: if the oracle hadn't foretold that Oedipus would marry his own mother, he would never have left Corinth and therefore never encountered either his father at the crossroads or the Sphinx, and having never solved its riddle he would not have been crowned king of Thebes and would certainly never have married his mother.

It is this same power of prophecy that makes the labour and money markets – and all the people who make up those markets – prone to self-destruction, with terrible effects for millions. When Miriam, Maria and other entrepreneurs see wages and interest rates falling or low, they prophesy that economic activity will go down or remain slow and so avoid borrowing money and hiring workers, thus ensuring that wages and interest rates stay low or fall further and fulfilling their own prophecies. Instead of recovering, the economy falls victim to their pessimism, which only perpetuates itself and intensifies.

If only Sophocles were writing our financial columns and economics textbooks, the nature and causes of a market society's trials and tribulations would be so much easier to discern.

The human element

Houses, cars, food and entertainment bring their own rewards and are desirable in their own right. In contrast, hired labour and borrowed money are only means to an end. Entrepreneurs are forced to lease them in order to produce things of exchange value, but they would love to live their lives without ever having to hire a single worker or borrow a single penny.

If the economy is the engine of society and debt is its fuel, then labour is the spark, the life-breathing force that animates that engine, while money is the lubricant without which that engine would seize up. It is poignant that both have the capacity to drive the engine but also to bring it to a standstill and prevent it from starting again. Taken together, they prevent the smooth operation that unemployment deniers and their fellows believe in and rule out a simple world in which unemployment disappears if wages fall sufficiently and savings are turned into jobs and equipment if the interest rate finds its 'right' level.

You may now be wondering whether something might be done to tame and control these demons. Is there no way to break the cycles of self-fulfilling prophecy and self-perpetuating pessimism? The answer is: it ain't going to be easy. The demons that turn the labour and money markets into market society's scourges are an expression of some of the very things that make us human: our ability to reflect on our own and others' behaviour, to inhabit others' minds and predict their actions, and to know that for all our cleverness and wisdom we and others rarely resist the short-term impulse for self-preservation, however self-defeating it may ultimately prove to be. To reconcile the messy, contradictory, irrational and perverse behaviour of humans with the smooth functioning of an idealized economic machine would require a rethink and a reorganization of society every bit as radical as the transformation of the Great Reversal that took place in eighteenth-century Britain.

Nevertheless, we are in the midst of one right now. It is the process of mechanization and automation, of digitalization and artificial intelligence. Unfortunately, it would appear to be taking us in the opposite direction to a solution, for its aim is not to reconcile human and machine but to replace the first with the second. But while the human spirit may be the greatest victim of this change, it is likely to prove our salvation too.

6

Haunted Machines

On a pitch-black night in the very early years of the nineteenth century a group of friends, including the author Mary Shelley and the poet Lord Byron, gathered at a mansion in the Swiss countryside. All night long the sky flashed with lightning and the rain poured down. In the trembling candlelight, amid the various creaks and groans the villa emitted as it weathered the tempest, our group of writers decided to hold a contest: each of them would write a horror story, and then they would judge whose was the most terrifying of all.

Mary Shelley came up with the story of Doctor Victor Frankenstein, a good doctor who had set out to conquer death in an era when it lurked around every corner. Cholera, common flu and malnutrition were decimating populations. Victor, a formidable scientist, was determined to defeat death. When his beloved wife fell ill, his determination grew greater. To conquer death, he first needed to understand it, to work out what underpinned life and turned flesh and blood into a living human, so he began experimenting with corpses, stitching together their best-preserved parts – the organs of one, the head of another, the hands of a third, and so on. His idea was to use the magical power of electricity to breathe life into his creation. For if he could fashion a living body from these raw materials, he thought, conquering death would be nigh.

Suddenly, Doctor Frankenstein's creation stirred. It torturously came alive, rising from the operating table, standing up and walking on its own. Then, almost immediately, it began searching for affection. Victor, consumed by fear and loathing at what he had made, dashed off, abandoning his creation to its own devices.

Incapable of integrating into a hostile society, the monster Victor had created murdered scores of people as revenge for the abandonment and loneliness his creator had forced on him – among them Victor's own wife. Finally, once the good doctor had tracked it all the way to the North Pole in the hope of destroying it and thus taking responsibility for the menace to humanity he had fashioned, the monster turned on his creator, killing Doctor Frankenstein in an act of desperate self-preservation.

The Frankenstein syndrome

At the time Mary Shelley was writing, the Napoleonic wars in continental Europe had not yet ended. While market society was emerging in Britain, as well as in Amsterdam – the other centre of fully fledged commercial society – everywhere else it remained only a distant possibility.

Nonetheless, while Byron, Shelley and their friends may have been Romantics they had their finger on history's pulse. Shelley's far-seeing novel reflected the anxiety of a sensitive writer about the effects that technology would have on society.

In Chapter 3 we saw how profit became an end in itself because the very first entrepreneurs were driven into debt before they had even set production in motion. Without profit, they would have become slaves to their creditors – as Doctor Faustus ultimately became a slave to Mephistopheles. To earn profits they were compelled to compete against one another for customers. To win customers, they were driven to reduce the prices of their products. To reduce prices, they tried perpetually to squeeze more products out of the same quantity of waged labour. If feats of mechanical engineering or technological inventions conferred an advantage in this struggle for survival, then they were swiftly adopted.

James Watt's steam engine and the many other inventions that have followed became integral to market societies only because of the profit motive and the competition between profit-seeking entrepreneurs that market societies beget. Suppose for a moment that Watt had lived in ancient Egypt under the pharaohs and had invented his steam engine then. What would have become of it? Imagine that Watt secured an audience with the pharaoh to demonstrate his invention. The most he could have expected was that the ruler of Egypt would have been impressed and placed one or more of his engines in his palace, demonstrating to visitors and underlings how ingenious his empire was. In the absence of entrepreneurs competing for profits, and given the hundreds of thousands of slaves the pharaoh had at his beck and call, Watt's engine would never have been used to power farms or workshops, let alone factories.

At first, acquiring a new machine gave an entrepreneur an advantage over their competitors by increasing production per worker. But of course, as soon as every other entrepreneur did the same, that advantage was cancelled out. Soon enough, a further technological innovation was obtained, pioneered by one or two leading entrepreneurs and then eventually became the norm across the industry. Thanks to this endlessly self-perpetuating process, humankind has gradually gained a vast army of mechanical slaves, such that today there is barely a single aspect of our lives that is not served at some point by machines.

As they work away ungrudgingly for us, we may begin to dream of a time when every tiresome job is finally mechanized, allowing us to live a more comfortable life in a society without work or chores – a society a little like the one in *Star Trek*, in which humans explore the universe, engaging in philosophical discussions on the bridge of the Starship *Enterprise*, their food automatically popping out of a hole in the wall – a 'replicator' – along with almost anything else the crew need or desire, from clothes and tools to musical instruments and jewellery.

But hold on. Reality is not turning out that way, is it? Our creations – the machines installed in every factory, field, office and shop – have helped produce a great many products and have changed our lives utterly, but they have not eradicated poverty, hunger, inequality, chores or the anxiety about our future basic needs. Might they yet do so? In some senses, the opposite seems to be happening. Machines work away, producing astonishing products in vast quantities, but instead of this making our lives easier, we've become more stressed than ever. We may no longer chain children to factory looms, but just as every employer is forced by competition to adopt the latest innovation, so most of us feel chained to our technology, increasingly harassed by the need to keep pace with its demands.

Many of us now have lower-quality jobs than we used to and feel more insecure than ever – and more anxious still about our children finding a job that will allow them the privilege of slogging away precariously at a mindless task in order to keep a roof over their heads. In important ways, we resemble hamsters on their spinning wheels: no matter how fast we run, we are not really going anywhere. We might well conclude that the machines aren't slaving away for our benefit; at times it even seems like we're working furiously to maintain *them*.

In this light, Mary Shelley's novel might serve as an allegory: a warning to its nineteenth-century readers that, if they were not careful, instead of serving humanity technology would create monsters to enslave us, terrorize us, possibly even destroy us; that these creations born of human ingenuity – like the life that Doctor Frankenstein managed to conjure from bits of corpses – would turn against their creators with tragic results.

The stories we tell reveal a lot about us. Judging by the literature and cinema that have emerged since industrialization, from the *Sweet Porridge* tale by the Brothers Grimm and Goethe's *The Sorcerer's Apprentice* to films such as *Blade Runner* and *The Terminator*, we are very afraid of our creations. Of all of these stories, there is one work of science fiction that in my view stands as today's worthy successor to Mary Shelley's *Frankenstein*, at least as an allegory for the tendency of market societies to use technology in a way that enslaves instead of liberates us: *The Matrix*.

The Matrix *and* Karl Marx

The creature assembled from various parts of corpses by Victor Frankenstein murders humans because of its unbearable existential angst. The machines in the *Terminator* movies seek to exterminate humanity as part of their planetary takeover bid. *The Matrix*, however, goes further, depicting an Earth on which machines have already taken over but still try to keep us alive.

The reason the machines cannot afford to let us die out is that, before they took power, we humans had exhausted the Earth's energy resources and covered the planet in an impenetrable black cloud that blocks solar energy. The only power sources that remain are our human bodies. Having imprisoned us in special pods, where we are fed and watered like hydroponic plants, and from which the heat generated by our metabolism can be captured and harnessed to power their machine society, the machines have found that, even if we are fed all the right nutrients and kept in optimum conditions, humans encased in pods, denied interaction, hope and freedom, die quickly. That's why the machines create the Matrix: a computer-generated virtual reality that can be projected into the brains of the enslaved humans, allowing our minds to experience life as it was before any of this occurred, keeping us unaware of our state of absolute slavery and exploitation.

Great futuristic movies like *The Matrix* strike a nerve because they speak to us about the present. *The Matrix* is a reflection – a documentary through metaphor, you might say – of our times or at least of our anxieties. It reveals our fear of a mechanization so complete, of a commodification of our bodies and enslavement of our minds so successful, that we are no longer even aware of it, made oblivious to our reality by the very technologies that rule us. In fact, *The Matrix* expresses a fear that this may *already* have happened but we have no way of knowing if it has.

Karl Marx, the famed revolutionary thinker of the nineteenth century, once wrote that the produced means of production – machines – are the 'force we must bow to'. You might say that *The Matrix* depicts the perfection of this process: it shows us the kind of situation that Karl Marx believed the evolution of market society is pushing us towards. (The fact that Doctor Marx was particularly influenced by Shelley's *Frankenstein* should not surprise you; those who write well about the economy borrow their best ideas from artists, novelists, scientists.)

And yet, according to Marx there is what we might call a safety feature within our economy that should give us cause for hope: a tendency built into market economies and enhanced by the mechanization of labour to generate a crisis *before* machines take over completely from human labourers, which prevents the jettisoning of all human labour from the production of things.

The Icarus syndrome

Remember the tale of Icarus? How he misused the wings his father Daedalus made for him from wax and feathers to escape from King Minos' Labyrinth? Eventually Icarus flew too close to the sun, melting the wax, and he plummeted into the Aegean Sea.

Market societies are prone to similar folly. At first, they edge gradually, painfully, towards automation, not unlike Icarus at the beginning of his flight struggling to gain altitude, but step by step workers' labour is squeezed out of the production process as various new technologies, from the steam engines of the eighteenth and nineteenth centuries to the robots of today, are adopted. With every step the cost of producing, say, a bolt of cloth or a car falls a little further, and competition between cloth or car manufacturers forces prices to fall too. But at some point technological change truly takes off, heading for the sun. The cost of producing a microchip or an iPhone starts to fall dramatically. We are at this stage already. Today if you visit a modern car plant or the latest smartphone or laptop factory, you'll see armies of mechanical robots working away with minimal human intervention. But as we know, the market society driving this process feeds off profits, and of course profits can only accrue if prices remain above costs. The problem is that three forces lead to prices falling below that level.

First, the automation of production pushes costs down. Second, the ruthless competition between producers stops them from charging prices above their (falling) costs. This has the effect of squeezing profits to a bare minimum. Third, the robots that have replaced human workers do not spend money on the products that they help produce. This has the effect of reducing demand. According to Marx, these three forces eventually lead prices to drop below the level necessary to cover costs and keep the whole thing going. That's the moment when, like Icarus, market society finds its wings melting. With automation happening at the furious pace that it is today, the likelihood of prices plunging more quickly than companies can cope with is all the greater.

In practice it unfolds like this. Faced with collapsing prices, entrepreneurs who have been forced by their competitors to borrow value from the future in order to invest in the latest machines discover that the profits on which they had been counting are disappearing. When the prices of many products fall below costs at the same time, some entrepreneurs, the weakest and least efficient, make the largest losses and go broke. They call their bankers with the awful news that they will not be able to meet their loan repayments and this sparks the cascade of consequences we discussed earlier: the economy crashes and the crisis hits.

We have seen all this before, except that now we have stumbled upon a deeper cause of crisis: the diminution, the squeezing out, of humanity from the production process. Yet it is at this moment that human labour makes its comeback, reclaiming at least a small part of the production process from the machines. How exactly?

The crisis forces both humans and machines into idleness: redundancy. It is at this point that any entrepreneurs who have managed to stay in business realize two things. One is that, with many of their competitors having closed down, competition has diminished. This allows them to raise prices a bit above costs, giving them a little boost. The other is that it is now cheaper to hire workers than to employ machines – possibly because of humans' problematic habit of needing to eat, which leads them to accept, at some point, any price for their labour. The result is that in the midst of the slump human workers regain some of their lost appeal in the eyes of employers and so recover some of the ground previously lost to machines. Indeed, during the worst global slump in living memory – which followed the crash of 2008 – workers made this kind of comeback in large swathes of the international market economy.

It is sometimes said that the most vengeful gods grant us our most intense desires. Employers' most intense desire is to eliminate the troublesome human element from their businesses while maintaining ownership of their machines' products and profiting from this monopoly. Any god that grants this wish must be truly vengeful. Like Midas, whose wish that all he touched would turn into gold left him sad and lonely, unable to touch his beloved lest he killed them, profit-hungry employers find that automation has the opposite effect to the one they hope for: loss of profit and, worse still, a crisis that may well bankrupt them.

Another allegory with which to describe the plight of market society is the well-known story of Sisyphus, the king condemned by Zeus to push a rock up a hill, only to see it roll all the way down just before it reached the summit, again and again, ad infinitum. Market societies are similarly condemned constantly to struggle to do something that unravels just before it is realized: to take the human element out of commodity production.

I don't know about you, but I find something soothing in this irony.

Resistance is never futile

At around the time when Mary Shelley was writing *Frankenstein*, a band of English workers known as the Luddites protested against the loss of their jobs to the new steam-powered looms in cotton and wool mills by destroying the machines. The Luddites are among history's more misunderstood protagonists. Their quarrel was not with the machines themselves, even though they wrecked quite a few of them; they were opposed to the fact that so few owned the machines. It was the social arrangement not the technology they objected to.

What the Luddites could not achieve – limiting the machines' onward march – has been achieved, at least sporadically, by market society's Icarus moments – those moments in history when a crash brought about by the combination of automation and bankers turned into a slump. This means that while automation continues to gather pace at an astonishing rate, it is only part of the picture.

If you were to catch a plane to Bangladesh today to visit a T-shirt-making facility, you would be startled to find thousands of workers, not machines, piecing together garments. The scene would be strikingly similar to the one depicted in Charlie Chaplin's 1936 movie *Modern Times*. In it Chaplin's character is a factory worker on a continuously moving assembly line, an innovation that had revolutionized production since its invention in 1913. Forced to work faster and faster to keep up with the machines, he soon starts to behave something like a machine himself, spirals out of control and causes such chaos that he ends up out of a job and in jail.

Judging by the continued existence of sweatshops at the same time as futuristic robotic factories, Marx seems to have been right, at least in one respect: our market society's particular take on technological innovation is not just a question of *replacing* workers with robots, it also involves *mechanizing* human workers when their wage makes them more attractive than robots.

And here we encounter another irony that should provide some hope for humans in the race against machines. Employing humans always comes with the advantage that workers, unlike machines, recycle their wages, however small they may be, helping to ensure there is a market for the T-shirts and other products they assist in producing. By the same token, if those wages fall – as happens when work becomes more mechanical and less skilled – there will come a point when they are too low to support the sales of the goods they help produce.

Looked at in this light, it is in the interests of all market society – including even employers in the overall balance

– for workers to resist their own mechanization, for it is this alone that puts the brakes on the profit-destroying process of automation. It is another paradox hidden in the foundations of market societies that although most employers are dead against it, the workers' capacity to organize themselves, especially through trade unions, to demand shorter hours, higher wages and more humane conditions, is the antidote to the Icarus syndrome.

In *Star Trek* our heroes often find themselves confronting the hordes of the Borg, a mechanized collective entity whose aim is to turn every species they encounter into one of their own and whose message to humans is 'You will be assimilated – resistance is futile!' On the contrary: resistance is *never* futile!

Machine-slaves or machine-masters?

You may remark that to automate production fully we would need to develop machines that can design and build new machines. This is correct. These days the greatest exchange value is produced by designers, not production-line workers or foremen. To give you one practical example, of the approximately £600 that an iPhone costs to buy, less than £150 goes to the factory that built it in China. The rest is kept by Apple as payment for its so-called intellectual property (IP) rights. So, all our speculation about a fully automated world like the one in *The Matrix* is pointless if human ingenuity, the capacity to innovate, to design machines and goods that do not currently exist, cannot be reproduced by machines. Can machines develop sufficiently to accomplish such tasks? Much depends on the answer to this question.

If they can, then we can envisage a process of production run entirely by an army of sophisticated android workers who work not only as manual labourers but also as inventors, designers and managers of all the various chores that humanity needs doing. We humans, meanwhile, would all be able to live like Socrates, Plato and Aristotle, chatting in the agora about the meaning of everything – except that in this futuristic scenario no human would be forced to do all those nasty jobs that the women and slaves of antiquity had to do. Alternatively, we may end up as human batteries encased in pods, oblivious to our enslavement.

Until either scenario comes about, what we *do* know is that machines will soon be doing extraordinary things, things that we cannot even begin to imagine now. In the next few years, for instance, it will be very hard to tell when speaking on the phone to some service provider whether you are talking to a human or to a machine. This will destroy many millions of jobs worldwide. The real question is: will these jobs be replaced by new ones that only humans can do well?

If our society remains organized as it currently is, with a tiny minority owning the right to receive the profits generated by machines, then I doubt it. In our far-from-ideal world, which contrasts so sharply with that of *Star Trek*, those in control of technology are determined to use it in order to increase their own profits and enhance their own power. Every employer's dream, after all, is not a society in which no one needs to work, profit is meaningless and each enjoys equally a commonwealth serviced by machines designed and directed by other machines. Their dream is having replaced all *their* workers with androids but no one else having done the same, allowing them to accumulate the profit and power unavailable to their competitors, who instead provide the market for their products by continuing to employ workers.

If I am right in this, our market societies will not evolve naturally into the good, *Star-Trek*-like society that the giant technology corporations insist they are bringing about. I fear that something more like *The Matrix* awaits us, controlled not by machines but by the fantastically wealthy and powerful heads of those companies. If so, it is not just a matter of waiting patiently until the Googles, the Apples, the Teslas, the Amazons and the Microsofts of today and tomorrow deliver a brave, new, wonderful world to us on a silver platter.

So what should we do instead?

The secret to exchange value: humans

In the last couple of decades an interesting new argument has surfaced. Given that the triumph of artificial intelligence over human intelligence is inevitable, then rather than changing the organization of our society, with its laws and rights over property, in order to halt or slow this process and preserve our doomed humanity, let's do the opposite: let's embrace the change and strive towards technologies that allow us to become 'post-human', indistinguishable from the sophisticated machines that are on their way. In other words, if you can't beat them, join them.

To understand fully the implications of this controversial vision we need first to answer a question: how does a human with a will or spirit of her own differ from an advanced robot?

In the 1982 film *Blade Runner* the protagonist, Rick Deckard (played by Harrison Ford), has the difficult and unpleasant task of detecting and destroying human-like robots that have escaped from faraway extraterrestrial colonies – where they were confined by humans fearful of their strength and intelligence – and found their way back to Earth. The problem is that as android technology has improved, these 'replicants' have become increasingly sophisticated and indistinguishable from humans. In Los Angeles' swarming sea of humanity Deckard finds it harder and harder to detect his targets, and when the latest, most advanced android model begins to develop emotions and a desire for freedom, Rick's task becomes inhumanly difficult. In *Blade Runner* Rick – and the viewer – is forced to ask what it means to be human.

Now suppose you were deaf and had a hearing aid fitted or, say, that your foot was replaced with a bionic one. Would you still be human? Of course you would. Suppose we then start replacing your organs, one after another, with mechanical ones: a bionic heart, mechanical lungs, artificial liver and kidneys. Are you still human now? Of course you are. What if now we move on to the brain? What if, for example, we place a microchip in a strategically located part of your brain – as is done to alleviate the symptoms of patients suffering Parkinson's disease – in order to improve your reflexes? Again, I suppose, behind all this technology you will be the same old Xenia.

But what if we then replace another bit of your brain? And another? And another? To cut to the chase, if we keep going, at some point something will be replaced in you that means you are no longer you, and ultimately there will come a point when you will indeed have become an android. We might not be able to define exactly which component, when replaced in you or me, tips us over the edge. It's enough to know, if only by its absence, that it exists.

Now suppose we did this not just to you but to all of the humans in the world as well. This would be as if everyone in the world of *Blade Runner* was actually a replicant – including Rick Deckard – or indeed as if we had not been enslaved by the Matrix but had become the machines that run it: a desirable state of affairs for those who envision a post-human future. Leaving aside whatever squeamish, sentimental objections you might have to such a future, I'm afraid that in purely economic terms a society of androids like this would be impossibly flawed.

Let us return to *The Matrix* and ask what is the main difference between the economy there and our kind of economy? The answer is that in our economy everything relies on exchange value, whereas in that of *The Matrix* the very concept of exchange value is nonsensical, meaningless. Yes, there is a complex economy in the world of *The Matrix*: an entire army of machines is required to maintain it, continuously replacing their own machine parts with improved ones, designing new technologies, producing new machines, and updating the Matrix. But without any self-aware humans equipped with judgement and free will, it no longer makes sense to speak of the machines' exchanges as having any value, for there is no one there to value them.

Consider for a moment an old mechanical clock. Each of the gears and springs inside it operates independently and in unison to produce the right time of day. It's a system full of complicated exchanges of energy. But to say that its parts create exchange value for one another is surely silly. Inhabiting the world of *The Matrix* or a post-human world populated only by replicants would be like inhabiting the insides of a clock or your laptop: a system of interrelating machine components operating without human intervention, capable of building marvellous structures, patterns, cities even, but incapable of producing exchange value.

These city-states would be more like beehives than societies, their members more like bees than citizens. It could no longer be said to be a market society. It might not even be a society at all.

Sources of hope

Like it or not, it is only a matter of time before technology actually creates human replicants capable of doing the vast majority of work. But while the post-human world is as unappetizing as it is incapable of supporting an economy, the solution cannot be the opposite either: to stop technological innovation that can free us of life's drudgery, generate clean energy and synthesize life-saving drugs. Let me be clear on this: I love technology and the immense benefits it can provide to humans and the planet, just as Mary Shelley, I am sure, loved the idea of science defeating disease. But it is one thing to love technology and another to stay complacently on the sidelines of history while human beings are turned gradually into the power generators of *The Matrix* – not least because that undermines the very thing that keeps the economy alive.

But who can prevent the unstoppable drive to mechanize production from causing crisis after crisis, condemning generation after generation of workers to underemployment or even fully fledged joblessness?

Who can appear as the Ghost of Christmas Yet to Come and warn the Ebenezer Scrooges of our mechanizing world of the future they are working towards?

Ironically, with technology advancing as it is, we may find that we are not alone in the struggle to keep the human spirit in the driving seat. In *Blade Runner*'s final scene Rick Deckard falls in love with an android that has developed emotions – one of those he was meant to terminate. Realizing that he would be in danger of losing his own humanity were he to kill the replicant, Deckard decides to disobey his own 'programming', elope with her and allow his android lover to find her own, indeterminate spirit. Such things may of course prove impossible in reality, but in a society determined to turn us into androids the idea that not only will we resist but that androids may also overcome their mechanical nature offers a glimmer of hope that technology won't necessarily lead to a dystopian *Matrix*; that something closer to *Star Trek* is feasible.

Setting aside such far-fetched sources of hope, let me now turn to the great, realistic hope close at hand: the belief, at least *my* belief, that humans have an inexhaustible ability to resist the erosion of their spirit and the cheapening of their labour. After all, *The Matrix* is not a story of enslavement; it is a story of our resistance to and escape from enslavement. The other source of hope is the knowledge that we have a fantastic ally in this struggle: should the process of automation ever be *too* successful, an Icarus-like crash is bound to ensue, putting paid to it.

We must of course never forget that crises destroy the lives of millions, of whole generations, and are never to be wished for. At the same time, our economy's periodic earthquakes offer opportunities for a revival of human labour. Bankruptcies and crises make it cheaper, at least for a while, for surviving businesses to employ destitute workers in place of expensive new robots. Every crisis is pregnant with a recovery. And vice versa.

A new and different Great Transformation

There is another benefit that crashes bring too. Well before you were born, during the so-called good times when turbocharged bank-created debt was powering the almighty bubble that eventually burst in 2008, conversation at dinner tables, in the media, in Parliament was delusional: middle-class people talked endlessly of the rising price of their home, their successful investments, their conviction that crises were a thing of the past. It was a sad and infuriating period. Though I was appalled and outraged at the suffering that followed the 2008 crash, I remember also how relieved I was when the bubble burst: at last the truth of our situation was clear. Humility could return.

Of course it is maddening that the only way we can preserve the human spirit and common sense is through periodic sacrifices on the bloodstained altar of economic crises. This is why we need to get on with a new and different Great Transformation, ensuring that the labour of machines is used wisely and benefits all. So what might that look like?

Here is one idea for how to align humanity's interests with the rise of the machines. Very briefly, this simple, practical measure would be for a portion of the machines of every company to become the property of everyone – with the percentage of profits corresponding to that portion flowing into a common fund to be shared equally by all. Consider what effect that would have on the course of human history.

Currently, increasing automation reduces the portion of total income that goes to workers, diverting more and more money into the pockets of the rich who own the machines. But as we have seen, this ultimately diminishes demand for their products, as the majority have less and less money to spend. But if a portion of the profits were to go automatically into the bank accounts of the workers as well, then this downward pressure on demand, sales and prices would be alleviated, turning the whole of humanity into the beneficiary of the machines' labour.

As long as highly skilled human labour remains necessary to design the machines that build other machines, full automation of the production process will not happen. In this scenario the effect of distributing profits as I have described would be to ensure that prices remain more or less stable while incomes rise, with the result that products become increasingly more affordable.

And if it ever happens that the production process *does* become fully robotized, with humans no longer needing to work on the design or the manufacture of the robots that make other robots, then all prices and all incomes will gradually recede until every product is like the air we breathe: so plentiful that no one needs to pay for it, however precious it may be. Then, and only then, we shall be able to boast, as *Star Trek*'s Captain Picard does, that 'People are no longer obsessed with the accumulation of things. We've eliminated hunger, want, the need for possessions. We have grown out of our infancy.'

Even though it may seem to you that I have lost the plot and succumbed to a science-fiction fantasy – as many will tell you I have – don't worry. I am in excellent company. In his essay on 'the economic possibilities for our grandchildren' one of the most highly regarded economists who ever lived, John Maynard Keynes, wrote the following: 'The love of money as a possession ... will be recognized for what it is, a somewhat disgusting morbidity, one of those semi-criminal, semi-pathological propensities which one hands over with a shudder to the specialists in mental disease.'

Even though he wrote this back in 1930 when the idea of fully robotized production was a lot more far-fetched than it seems today, Keynes sounds very much like Captain Picard, don't you think?

To put it as clearly and plainly as possible: we urgently need as a species a way to make full use of our technological potential without periodically destroying the livelihoods of great swathes of humanity and ultimately enslaving ourselves to the few. To do this, we must first and foremost redistribute between us the riches that the machines we have created can produce through part-ownership of those machines. I can think of no other way of turning human society from the slave of its creations into their master.

What stops us from doing this? The fierce opposition of the tiny but very powerful minority who own the existing machines, land, office blocks and of course the banks. What do we do in the face of their resistance?

In the final two chapters I hope to convince you that the answer to this most important question is the same whether we are examining the rise of machines – as we have in this chapter – or the lifeblood of the economy, money – as we shall in the next chapter – or the lifeline of our species, the environment – as we shall in the final chapter.

Bear with me. The answer will come soon enough.

7

The Dangerous Fantasy of Apolitical Money

During the Second World War the German authorities treated their prisoners of war differently, according to where they came from. Russians, the Roma and certainly the Jews they murdered. British, Commonwealth, American and French prisoners of war, on the other hand, they accorded the basic rights laid down by the internationally agreed Geneva Conventions.

In 1941 Richard Radford, an officer in the British army, was captured by German forces and placed in a camp for Western prisoners of war. When the war ended, Radford took the time to record his experience of life in the POW camp through the prism of his training as an economist.

In the camp prisoners of different nationalities were kept in different buildings, between which they were usually free to move about. The Red Cross oversaw their living conditions and supplied them with packages at regular intervals from its Swiss headquarters. These packages typically contained food, cigarettes, coffee, tea, a bar of chocolate and so on. The arrival of the Red Cross packages broke the monotony of life in the camp and was eagerly anticipated, especially by the smokers. Even though the prisoners' preferences varied considerably, in a rare instance of strict equality the packages were identical for all prisoners. The first to spot the opportunity to profit from these differences in taste were some shrewd French officers. Knowing that the average Frenchman loves coffee and doesn't care much for tea, while the opposite held for the average Englishman, they established a regular exchange of goods between prisoners of various nationalities.

Once the Red Cross truck had unloaded its cargo, the ingenious French traders approached their countrymen, borrowing from them the tea contained in their packages and promising an amount of coffee in return. Then they went to the buildings where the British prisoners were held and exchanged the tea for coffee, which they then returned to their French compatriots as they had promised. But why do this? What was in it for them?

The French traders' gain took the form of coffee that they kept for themselves. How did they manage that? By offering their compatriots less coffee for their tea than the Englishmen were prepared to hand over in exchange for that same quantity of tea.

Arbitrage

In economic terms the French traders were effectively paying their countrymen a lower price for the tea they bought from them than the price they charged the tea-loving Englishmen. Of course the price was measured – *denominated* – not in pounds, marks or dollars, since the inmates of the camp had no actual money, but in ounces of coffee. In economic parlance this practice of buying for a lower price in one market and selling for a higher price in another is called *arbitrage*.

Others quickly caught on and started doing the same. The greater the competition between the traders, the smaller the difference became between the quantity of coffee they offered the French prisoners in return for their tea and the quantity of coffee the Englishmen forked out for the tea they received in exchange. This difference – or *spread* – was where the traders' profit lay. The smaller the spread, the less profit they made.

Consider Pascal, a latecomer to the business. To convince his compatriots to give their tea to him and not to one of his more established competitors, Pascal is forced to offer them more coffee than they might normally receive in exchange for the same amount of tea. It is as if he is offering them a higher price for their tea. As others follow Pascal in order to gain or retain a foothold in the market, the price of tea in the French buildings continues to rise, squeezing the traders' (coffee) profits further. At the same time similar bargaining over prices is taking place in the English buildings, until finally it becomes common knowledge in the French buildings how much coffee their tea will buy in the English buildings, and it becomes common knowledge in the English buildings how much tea their coffee will buy in the French buildings.

At this point Pascal and all the other French traders can no longer get away with paying a little bit less coffee for their compatriots' tea than they receive from the English – everyone knows what their tea and coffee is worth. In other words, thanks to their efforts the traders have helped establish the price of tea and in the process done themselves out of a job.

Very quickly all sorts of goods were being traded across the camp, with most of the POWs participating in this spontaneous, multinational market in which each person sought to acquire as many comforts as they could in the camp's adverse conditions. As trade between prisoners developed, prices for all sorts of goods stabilized around what economists like to refer to as an *equilibrium*. Before the equilibrium had been reached, traders profited according to their bargaining skills and salesmanship – one might buy a chocolate bar for ten grams of coffee, while another might manage to sell a chocolate bar for fifteen grams of coffee – but as trading continued and competition shrank the spreads, prices stabilized, profits collapsed and skilled traders lost all advantage. Now they had to conjure up new types of trade – new markets in other words – if they were to exploit their trading skills.

This stabilization of exchange values, or relative prices, was helped along by the presence of noticeboards around the camp on which traders posted offers: for example, 'I'm selling 100 grams of coffee for 10 chocolate bars.' Prisoners could thus see at a glance the sort of prices available and would know not to accept nine chocolate bars for the same amount of coffee, helping to establish stable prices all over the camp. Have you noticed in movies or on TV those large screens that traders have in the trading rooms of banks or the stock exchange? These are so-called Bloomberg screens, on which the shifting prices for oil, gold, company shares and government bonds appear in real time, and are essentially more advanced versions of the noticeboards in Radford's POW camp. Their job is to facilitate trade and to eliminate spreads, getting rid of opportunities for arbitrage in the process.

The emergence of a carcinogenic currency: cigarettes

In time transactions in the camp became more complicated, and the system of direct exchanges – tea for coffee, coffee for chocolate – proved a drag.

Imagine, for example, that a Canadian is offering a hundred grams of coffee in exchange for ten bars of chocolate. A Frenchman who wants the coffee, doesn't have any chocolate but does have tea would have to do some research before proposing something like: 'I want your coffee, but I don't have chocolate. I do have tea, though, and I know this Scottish guy in building C5 who is offering fifteen grams of tea per chocolate bar. So how about you give me that hundred grams of coffee, and in return I give you a hundred and fifty grams of tea, which you can then exchange with the Scotsman for ten bars of chocolate?'

That's how things were in the beginning, but soon a significant change came about: one particular commodity became established as a go-between that could mediate the sale of all the other commodities. In effect, it became a currency. Obviously, cigarettes were among the best-selling goods in the camp. Smokers, courtesy of their addiction to nicotine, would sell their souls to the devil, so to speak, to get more of them. As a result non-smokers were at a great advantage, since their packages contained cigarettes too – cigarettes that had no experiential value for them but packed great exchange value. Immediately, cigarettes were in great demand both for their experiential value (to smokers) and for their exchange value (to everyone, including non-smokers).

It was only a matter of time before cigarettes were established as the unit for measuring exchange values, or relative prices, in the camps. Why cigarettes? Which goods end up evolving into a unit of currency has always depended partly on chance and partly on their having some basic properties. They must be durable so that they do not perish, unlike say bread or fish. They must be convenient to carry, preferably pocket sized. They must be easily divisible into smaller portions. And their appeal must be evenly spread throughout the community.

Radford's account relates how cigarettes were transformed from a simple, carcinogenic good into a special commodity with three distinct properties and roles. First, they were sources of the nicotine that smokers craved. Second, they functioned as a means of exchange and a measure allowing for an easy, immediate, comparison of prices. Third, cigarettes could be stashed away, offering prisoners the opportunity to create a nest egg of exchange value in the harsh conditions of the POW camp.

This last use of cigarettes, as a store of exchange value, is perhaps the most interesting as its repercussions extended beyond the realm of convenience and trade facilitation: by giving prisoners the opportunity to save for a rainy day, new opportunities and new risks emerged. One obvious opportunity was the possibility of lending one's saved cigarettes to another prisoner in return for interest. The risk that this brought was the possibility that the borrowing prisoner might not pay them back, known as the risk of *default*. For example, the borrower might spend all the cigarettes – or even smoke them all – and be unable to return them to the creditor.

But another risk came from elsewhere.

*The exchange value of money: inflation and
deflation in the POW camp*

When I was your age I recall hearing a grown-up saying
something that I could not get my head around. I just did
not get it, however hard I tried. Even when I thought I had
understood it, I tried to explain it to a friend and realized
that I hadn't. What was it that this grown-up had said?
That a one-thousand-drachma note (the currency we had
back then) cost only twenty drachmas to produce. *How
can it be worth a thousand drachmas*, I kept wondering,
when it only cost twenty?

Maybe you are smarter than I was, but humour
me nevertheless as I attempt to explain this puzzle
in the context of Radford's POW camp. Periodically,
the Red Cross would place a few more cigarettes
in the prisoners' packages but keep the quantity of
chocolate, tea and coffee the same. When the extra
cigarettes arrived at the camp, each cigarette now
bought less coffee, less chocolate and less tea. Why?
Because overall a larger number of cigarettes now
corresponded to the same amount of coffee and tea,
each individual cigarette corresponded to less coffee
and less tea. The opposite also held true: the fewer
cigarettes there were in comparison to the other goods
that the Red Cross placed in the packages, the greater
the exchange value, or purchasing power, of each
cigarette. In short, the purchasing power of a unit of

currency has nothing to do with how much it costs to produce but, rather, its relative abundance or scarcity.

Imagine that a prisoner has been hoarding his cigarettes in order to make a large purchase when suddenly the Red Cross sends tons of cigarettes to the captives. Suddenly, the exchange value of his cigarettes drops, and his parsimony and abstinence have been to no avail.

In this way we see how having access to a currency lubricates transactions no end, helping the economy move more commodities more quickly. On the other hand, for a currency to function it requires trust and faith: the trust that everyone will continue to accept it in return for any commodity, which is in turn based on faith that the currency's exchange value will be maintained. It is no coincidence that in your second language, Greek, the word for 'coin' (*nomisma*) straddles the verb 'to think' (*nomizo*) and the noun for 'law' (*nomos*). Indeed, what gives value to coins and paper money is the *legal obligation* to accept them across the realm and the *belief* that they are and will remain valuable.

One night Allied bombers hammered the area where the camp was located. The bombs landed closer and closer, some falling in the camp itself. All night long the prisoners wondered whether they would live to see daybreak. The next day the exchange value of cigarettes had gone through the roof! Why? Because over the course of that endless night, surrounded by exploding bombs and consumed by anxiety, the prisoners had smoked cigarette after cigarette. In the morning the total number of cigarettes had shrunk dramatically in relation to the other goods. If previously five cigarettes had been needed to buy one chocolate bar, now only one cigarette was needed to buy that same bar.

In short, the bombardment had caused what is known as *price deflation* – a decrease in all prices as a result of a reduction of the quantity of money in relation to all other goods. The opposite, a general increase in prices as a result of a larger quantity of money in the overall system, is known as *price inflation*.

Interest rates: the price of money in the camp

For all of 1942, when it was still impossible to tell how the war would end and the prisoners feared it might be many years before they'd be able to return to their homes, prices in the camp were relatively stable. Confident that the camp's primitive economy would remain in place for a while, some – those with the most business-savvy minds and the most accumulated wealth – began to function as, yes, bankers, offering loans in the expectation that they would get their savings back before death or liberty arrived.

If, say, Xavier ran out of coffee and didn't have enough cigarettes to buy more, he might go to one of these bankers and ask for a loan of ten cigarettes. The banker would offer to lend Xavier the cigarettes provided that next month, when his package from the Red Cross arrived, he promised to pay back twelve cigarettes in return – an exorbitant monthly interest rate of 20 per cent. Would Xavier agree? Yes, if he was pained more by the thought of waiting for a whole month before drinking coffee than by the prospect of having to do with two fewer cigarettes than he would otherwise have had afterwards.

Expected fluctuations in the overall quantity of money influenced interest rates significantly. For example, if the bankers anticipated that a large number of cigarettes would be sent to the camp in the coming month, causing their exchange value to fall and prices to inflate, they would increase the interest rate they charged. Why? Because they were afraid that one month later the same quantity of cigarettes would be worth less. This is why in any economy the cost of borrowed money – interest – depends on expectations of what prices will be, on inflation or deflation.

To give an example: a banker predicts that the exchange value of each cigarette will fall by 10 per cent – in other words, that inflation will occur, and the price of goods expressed in cigarettes will rise by 10 per cent. In the past he was ready to lend ten cigarettes in return for twelve next month. Now he calculates that a monthly interest rate of 20 per cent will result in an increase for him not of 20 per cent but of 20 per cent minus 10, which is only 10 per cent. (This figure is known, intuitively enough, as the *real* interest rate.) Understandably, if the banker wants to maintain his same level of profit, he won't be prepared to loan the cigarettes for 20 per cent any more. What would he accept? A rate of 30 per cent per month, adding 10 per cent to his normal interest rate in order to make up for the 10 per cent less that his money will be worth.

If you hear somebody in some boring news report remark, 'Interest rates will probably rise because inflation seems to be picking up,' you now have no excuse not to understand what they are going on about. Radford's POW camp is all you need …

Great expectations

The weather and other natural phenomena do not give a monkey's about what we think of them or what we predict they will do. If it is to rain, it will rain regardless of what the Met Office has said or what you and I expect. But as we know from Rousseau's stag hunt and from the two Oedipal markets, the economy, unlike nature, is influenced, buffeted and indeed shaped by what we think of it. Radford's POW camp demonstrates this interdependence superbly, with particular reference to the value of money.

News from the fronts had a particularly strong impact on the POW camp's economy. When the prisoners got word that the German army was making gains in Russia – often by listening to makeshift radios they had built behind their guards' backs – they assumed that they would remain captive for a very long time. As a result, prices tended to stabilize. But when they started to realize that the war was nearing its end, foreshadowing their liberation and the elimination of their little economy, the interest rates bankers offered to savers (rather than the ones they charged for loans) skyrocketed, since nobody wanted to save.

When the front lines reached the German border, packages from the Red Cross stopped arriving. Knowing the war was about to end, the prisoners smoked the cigarettes they had accumulated, and the debts that some of them still owed to the bankers literally went up in smoke. Before American troops had thrown the gates of the POW camp open, its remarkable little economy had collapsed.

From this it is clear that a monetized economy cannot be sustained if everyone knows its end is nigh. Everything relies on trust in its longevity as the very anticipation of collapse is enough, in an Oedipal fashion, to cause collapse.

This is true of all economies, from the one in Radford's POW camp to our own today. There are, however, fundamental differences between the way money worked in the camp and the way it works in our market societies. In the POW camp it was the Red Cross which was in control of the 'money' supply, although their staff probably knew nothing about any of this. They simply delivered what goods they could to the POWs, going about their humanitarian work without a thought for the camp's economy. In this sense the ultimate authority that ruled over the camp's money system was genuinely impartial.

Alas, in our market society, this is far from being the case.

From cigarettes to political money

Cigarettes have emerged as currency units in concentration camps and jails the world over; for those at liberty there is a wider choice of materials to choose from. Shells, salt and precious metals such as iron have all been used. Gold's magical chemical properties, which prevent it corroding and allow it to retain its shine, has made it an all-time favourite. When paper currency first replaced metal coins, at least for larger values, people were shocked – just as I found it hard to understand how a piece of paper that cost twenty drachmas to manufacture could be worth a thousand. Since then, as notes have grown smaller and lighter, currency has grown less and less tangible, even dematerializing altogether; today we are increasingly au fait with the idea of transferring currency via an app on our smartphone. But as with the cigarettes in Radford's camp, what makes a currency function – what gives it *currency* – is trust.

Since ancient times rulers have had to protect the people's trust in their currency, often from their own greed. In Mesopotamia, as we saw, the inscribed shells that acted as receipts for grain owed to farmers as well as units of currency would have lost their credibility instantly if the ruler had issued promises of an implausible quantity of grain or had failed to control the officials who provided the shells and wrote the numbers on them. The same applied to coinage, where the issue was how much of a precious metal (like gold or silver) they contained. Counterfeiters had every incentive to melt coins down and remake them with less gold or silver, keeping the difference. The widespread scepticism this practice caused impeded transactions, as people thought twice before accepting a coin purporting to have a certain exchange value that it might lack.

To counter the scepticism, the authorities stamped their coins with an image, usually that of the ruler, as a guarantee that the coins in circulation were under the sovereign's constant watch. In ancient Athens, for example, the city-state had strict rules and official testing centres at ports and around markets that used advanced technical methods to perform random testing of coins –

as well as of other commodities such as wine, ensuring its purity and alcoholic content. The punishments for trafficking counterfeit coins were grave, ranging from whipping all the way to execution. And since prevention is preferable to punishment, increasingly complex designs depicting feared gods or tyrants were used on the coins in the hope of staying one step ahead of the counterfeiters.

That was all well and good but, as the old phrase goes, 'Who will protect us from our protectors?' The power to issue currency often proved too much for fallible rulers to enjoy without abuse. The incentives they faced to short-change the public were powerful ones. Every time they wanted to wage a war or build a new temple or palace, the temptation to reduce the amount of precious metal that went into the coins so as to produce more of them proved hard to resist.

Their subjects were not stupid, of course: they learned how to distinguish between the older and the newer coins. But it did not take long for the bad coins to drive the good coins out of circulation, as people hoarded the good ones or melted them down to obtain their relatively plentiful silver or gold. But with so much additional and debased currency in circulation, each coin came to be worth less wheat, less corn, less meat. Price inflation took hold; people found their wages and savings losing value, and the economy faltered, even throwing the entire currency into jeopardy if trust in it failed entirely. The decline of the Roman empire, for instance, was riddled with such episodes.

It is therefore quite understandable that many people feel that their rulers, their government, their politicians cannot be entrusted with such decisions, which should be kept as far away as possible from the machinations of power-hungry men – and yes, it was and remains mostly men who have stuck their snouts into the common trough.

Times have thankfully changed to some extent. Through a series of insurrections the rule of law was imposed upon the rulers by the ruled, limiting the extent to which the king could plunder his subjects, impose taxes at will, confiscate their land and incarcerate them when they resisted. Taxes became something much more than a levy on the poor for the further enrichment of the powerful. In response to popular movements demanding a fairer division of the surplus, taxes became a source of funding for various projects benefiting broader segments of the population. Even the rich began to realize that a welfare state was an excellent insurance policy against losing their property, their peace of mind, indeed their own heads. But the question then became: who pays for this? As we have previously noted, the rich never like to pay the necessary taxes and the poor cannot afford to. So what then?

One option, as we saw in Chapter 4, was deficit-financed state expenditure – or public debt. Another was to create more money, either via the banks or via the central bank that the state instituted to fund itself and to fund the bankers in their hour of need. Both options have their demerits. Politicians dislike increases in public debt because their opponents go to town against them, accusing the government of condemning their children to a future of higher taxes in order to pay it off. One tendency therefore is quietly to instruct the central bank to create more money with which to pay for the things that society so badly needs.

But just as the POWs in Radford's camp who had accumulated large stashes of cigarettes disliked the arrival of new cigarettes from the Red Cross as they diminished the purchasing power of their own, so the moneyed classes have always bitterly resisted this solution. Citing the fall of the Roman empire, attributed partly to the failing Roman emperors' debasement of the currency, the wealthy went on a campaign to 'depoliticize' central banks and make them independent of government – taking away the politicians' power to instruct the central bank to increase the money supply. But leaving aside for now the question of whether it is really desirable to depoliticize money in this way, is it even possible?

The difference between the POW camp economy and monetized market economies

To answer this question, let us begin by noting another difference between Radford's POW camp economy and our own. In the camp currency was money and money was currency – the stock of cigarettes acting as the stock of currency, and the stock of currency being the only money that existed. However, outside the POW camp's barbed wire the volume of money massively exceeds the quantity of coins and paper notes in circulation. Why is this?

The short answer is: thanks to the bankers' magical power to create money from nothing. As you will remember, when Miriam received her loan of half a million pounds it simply appeared in her bank account; it never took the form of currency, of coins or paper notes. But it was money nonetheless, which she used in order to purchase the equipment that she needed for her bicycle workshop. This is possible in market societies because Miriam will go on to produce bicycles worth half a million pounds, plus a bit extra to pay the bank its interest and earn a profit on top. In the POW camp, by contrast, there was no production, only consumption, and without production there is no way of turning debt into profit in this way. Such a thing would have been more or less impossible. From this perspective, the camp's economy was a fully fledged market but nothing like a market society, since nothing that the POWs consumed was produced within it.

Let us also recall how this magical power of the bankers to create money and the overall demands of a market society generate an urgent need for public debt – the ghost in the machine, as I described it. It is public debt that pays for the infrastructure on which the whole functioning of the economy depends, that boosts the recycling process when it slows, that provides over-excitable bankers with their 'most liquid of assets', that is the elastic band that holds everything together when they get carried away. In turn, public debt engenders a new urgency in the state to collect taxes, if only to keep repaying part of the public debt. The crucial difference between the economy in Radford's POW camp and the economies of market societies is that in the former debt and taxes were unrelated to the supply of money whereas in the latter they are inextricably linked.

After all, physical currency did not originally come about in order to facilitate exchanges, as it did in Radford's camp. It was invented to record debts – debts that the rich rulers used in order to pay poor farmers like Mr Nabuk – and to collect taxes. (Hence, while rulers have always been tempted to debase the currency in order to profit themselves, they have always been restrained from doing so by the knowledge that it would reduce the value of the taxes they received.)

If money were to be depoliticized, if its supply were to be separated from the world of politics, then we can now see that all of the following decisions would have to be made independently of politics: how much government spends and on what; how much tax the state collects and from whom; what bankers should be allowed to get away with; how to deal with bankers when they go bankrupt. To the extent that these decisions are the very definition of politics, then they can be undemocratic if they are taken by the oligarchy, but they can never be apolitical.

Once more let me remind you why money in Radford's POW camp was apolitical: because its supply came from an independent source, the Red Cross, which did not know it was providing Radford and his fellow POWs with a currency. Everywhere else the authorities in control of the money supply know full well the power they have over our economy. In such a position, given that they know the likely consequences of their decisions, the question is not whether they should act dispassionately – they cannot – the question is whether they should act in the interests of the many or the few.

It is the case that the central banks of almost all of the world's economically advanced democracies are formally independent. In each of these countries has money been depoliticized now that the central bank is no longer under the purview or influence of elected politicians? Given that money is inextricably bound up with the institutional management of debt (public and private) and taxation – an entirely political affair – the answer is no. What really happens when the central bank becomes independent of elected politicians is this: rather than having a central bank as neutral as the Red Cross, we end up with a central bank whose decisions remain as political as ever, except that they are no longer supervised by Parliament. As a result, they end up more dependent than ever on the political and financial might of the powerful unelected few: the oligarchy and the bankers.

An attempt to depoliticize money: Bitcoin

Now let me take you back to 2008, to that moment in recent history when you were only four and when the bankers' bubble burst spectacularly. The loss of so many jobs and homes and hopes imbued Western societies with unprecedented distrust of the money lords – the private bankers, the politicians in charge of our market economy and the theoretically independent central bankers in charge of the money supply. As central bankers from the twenty richest countries, the so-called G20, got together to agree on how to rescue the bankers, citizens around the world were incensed. Some began to dream of a new kind of currency, one not dissimilar to the cigarettes in Radford's POW camp: de-nationalized, apolitical and beyond the reach of the high and mighty; a currency created *by* the people, *for* the people, which neither bankers nor the state could manipulate.

Who would issue the currency and regulate its quantity and quality if not a government or central bank?

Such questions were unanswerable before the digital age, but since the Internet arrived, the vision of a democratic, safe and honest digital currency with no physical form, existing only in our computers and smartphones, independent of any central control, has been growing in progressive minds with an anti-authoritarian bent. The challenge has always been this: unlike a banana or a hundred-dollar note, which I cannot eat or spend twice, anything digital is just a string of numbers sitting on a hard drive and can therefore be copied and multiplied by anyone. If there's nothing to stop me or you from creating as much currency as we want, how can we keep tabs of how much each one of us has the right to spend? Without a solution to this problem, a digital currency would immediately be destroyed by mistrust and hyper-price inflation.

A brilliant answer to this question was sent in an email to an online chatroom on 1 November 2008, a few weeks after the crash hit. The email was signed by Satoshi Nakamoto, a pseudonym hiding a person or team whose identity hasn't been uncovered to this day. In this email Nakamoto presented a dazzling computer program – an algorithm – that solved this problem and would become the basis for a new decentralized digital currency – the so-called Bitcoin.

Before Nakamoto's email all other solutions required a central authority of some kind. Banks and credit card companies like Visa or Mastercard deal with the problem by creating a central digital spreadsheet. Every time you pay for something on Amazon using my credit card, a number of dollars is taken out of the entry in that central spreadsheet – or ledger – next to my name and account number and is put next to Amazon's name and account number on the same central spreadsheet. Before every purchase I make, the central system checks to see that there are sufficient funds next to my name, ensuring I never spend the same money twice.

The beauty of Nakamoto's algorithm was that it did away with the ledger run by a central authority but still managed to ensure that a single currency unit could never be copied or spent twice. 'Who would take responsibility for policing transactions then?' I am sure you want to ask. The fascinating answer is everyone! The whole community using Bitcoin would share in the task by each making available a small part of their computer's capacity for this purpose. Everyone would observe everyone else's transactions, ensuring their validity, while at the same time no one would know whose transactions they were observing, safeguarding privacy. Many people around the world were enthused and signed up.

Bitcoin experienced some terrible teething problems. Despite the fact that nobody was able to crack Nakamoto's algorithm, a handful of malevolent entrepreneurs exploited people's fears that their computers might be hacked, with the hackers escaping with the strings of digits that are their hard-earned Bitcoins. These entrepreneurs offered Bitcoin-rich customers a service: safeguarding their Bitcoins by storing (electronically) their strings of digits on super-safe servers, charging a small fee in return. Yes, you guessed it: one or two unscrupulous safeguarders then disappeared into the night with other people's Bitcoins worth several million dollars.

What is truly interesting about this story is that it reminds us why money is, and must always be, political. That money is political is not something Bitcoin's supporters dispute. Their love for Bitcoin and other so-called cryptocurrencies stems from what they see as its anarchic, anti-establishment, counter-authoritarian nature. This is as political as it gets. What Bitcoin supporters would not like, however, is what I am going to say next: that money can be kept separate from the state and from the political process leading to the formation of our governments and their policies is a dangerous illusion.

The dangerous fantasy of apolitical money

When the scandal over the large-scale theft of Bitcoins erupted, many saw in it proof the currency was flawed because no one protects people using it from fraud and theft. If robbers break into a normal bank and leave with millions, the law ensures that your deposits are safe, but with Bitcoin being outside the jurisdiction of any state, no one will come to your rescue.

This lack of a state-backed insurance scheme for users is a serious fault, no doubt. We might dislike it, but the state is ultimately our only insurance policy against organized crime. However, this is not the most serious weakness of stateless currencies like Bitcoin. Their greatest and most dangerous weakness is that, because they are founded on the notion that no intervention in the money supply should be possible lest this intervention be manipulated by governments or bankers, it is impossible to adjust the total quantity of money in the system in response to a crisis – and this makes a crisis worse, as we have seen.

Bitcoin's algorithm specifies that the number of Bitcoins in existence is essentially fixed. (To be more precise, the quantity grows slowly until it reaches a maximum number – 21 million Bitcoins, to be precise – some time in 2032.) But this is very problematic for two reasons: first, it makes a crisis more likely and, second, it makes it harder to alleviate the crisis when it hits.

Let's first see why the fixed quantity of Bitcoins makes a crisis more likely: its so-called deflationary effect. As businesses create more products, each Bitcoin will become relatively scarcer and so be worth more and more. Which means that the price, measured in Bitcoins, of each car or gadget falls even faster than the pace dictated by automation. And this will happen across the board: price deflation. This is not a problem in and of itself but becomes a huge one if wages fall faster than prices, meaning workers can only afford to buy fewer of the multiplying products. This fall in sales due to Bitcoin's deflationary effect adds a destabilizing factor to the bankers' standard overexuberance and sparks a crash more readily.

Once the crash has happened, the second problem of a Bitcoin-powered economy emerges: the impossibility of reflating the economy by increasing the quantity of money. After a crash, when the money bankers had conjured up from the future fails to materialize, the government must replace some of that missing money quickly, bailing out banks (though not the bankers) and spending on the poor, on public works and so on.

Unless it takes swift action to increase the money supply, the chain reaction of insolvencies will push everyone into a 1930s-like slump. But such swift action is not possible under Bitcoin, whose supply is fixed and outside the authorities' grasp.

None of this is speculation. It is what happened before and after the crash of 1929, when governments were determined to keep the money supply in unchanging proportion to the amount of gold they possessed – a policy known as the Gold Standard, which is very close in spirit to the aversion to political money that lies behind Bitcoin. It was only after the British government in 1931 and President Roosevelt's so-called New Deal government in 1933 decoupled the quantity of currency from gold holdings that some relief came.

But of course, as soon as someone such as a government or a central bank manages the money supply, political money has returned.

A concluding remark

To recap: controlling the money supply is our only faint hope of charting a course that avoids the Scylla of bubbles, debt and unsustainable development on the one hand, and the Charybdis of deflation and stagnation on the other. But as any such intervention will affect different people – the rich and propertied on the one hand, the poor and powerless on the other – in different ways, it can never be impartial. Having accepted that money is inescapably political, there is only one thing we can do to civilize it: democratize it! Give the power to control it to the people on the basis of one person, one vote. It is the only defensible way we know.

Of course, to democratize our money we will need to democratize our states first. And this is a tall, tall order. But it may not be impossible. When I finished writing this chapter, I asked your grandfather, my dad, if cigarettes had ended up becoming currency units in the camps on the islands of Makronissos and Ikaria where he spent several years as a political prisoner during the Greek Civil War of 1946–9. I suppose I was asking partly in order to find out how universal Radford's POW story might be. His answer surprised me, I must say.

'No,' your grandfather said. 'We shared whatever packages each of us received. Once, despite the fact that I didn't smoke, I asked my aunt to send me cigarettes. As soon as I received them, I passed them on to others who smoked without expecting anything from them in return. That's how it was. We helped each other out.'

There is a lesson somewhere here but I shall leave it to you to tease out.

8

Stupid Viruses?

In *The Matrix* a small band of humans have managed to escape their enslavement by the machines and are at large, resisting the machines' efforts to recapture them. Their leader is a man called Morpheus. At one point in the film Morpheus is captured by the machines within the virtual reality of the Matrix, which appear in the human form of a character called Agent Smith. Before Agent Smith brutally interrogates Morpheus, 'he' explains why humans sicken 'him': 'You see, every mammal on this planet instinctively develops a natural equilibrium with their surrounding environment, but you humans do not … There is another organism on this planet that follows the same pattern. Do you know what it is? A virus. Human beings are a disease, a cancer of this planet. You are a plague. And we are the cure.'

Judging from the three great monotheistic religions – Judaism, Christianity and Islam – we humans think very highly of ourselves. We like to think that we've been fashioned in the image and likeness of God, of that which is perfect and unique. As the only mammal endowed with the gifts of speech and reason, we consider ourselves to be demi-gods, masters of the Earth, and to have the ability to adapt our environment to our desires instead of our having to adapt to it. That's why we get flustered by the thought of a machine – one of our creations – turning round and speaking to us as Agent Smith speaks to Morpheus. Worst of all, deep down, we're afraid that Agent Smith is right.

I might even go so far as to say that he's being particularly lenient on us. After all, there are some viruses that do not destroy their host cells, whereas we seem wholly intent on destroying our host environment. We've driven plants and animals to mass extinction, destroyed two thirds of the planet's forests, created acid rain that poisons its lakes, eroded the soil and dammed or drained rivers completely, pumped our atmosphere full of carbon dioxide, which is acidifying our oceans and killing its reefs, melting the ice caps, raising sea levels, destabilizing the climate and endangering entire peoples. We've so jeopardized the biosphere, our only refuge, that we resemble – and in a literal sense actually are – astronauts who poison their own oxygen supply. Who can doubt that Agent Smith is right?

You'll tell me – and you've got every right to – that Agent Smith doesn't exist. That he's the figment of some screenwriters' imagination. Just as Christopher Marlowe created Doctor Faustus and Mary Shelley created Doctor Frankenstein in order to awaken our consciences and raise the alarm, maybe the existence of Agent Smith as a fiction proves that we are not a mere cancer or virus threatening the planet, that we are a species with a conscience, one capable of self-criticism and reflection.

The question is whether we shall prove capable of making these noteworthy virtues count.

Exchange value vs Planet Earth

Market societies made their appearance as exchange values were triumphing over experiential values. As we have seen, it was a triumph that produced unimaginable wealth and untold misery and led to mass mechanization, exponentially increasing the quantity of products humanity could fabricate while turning workers and employers alike into the machines' mechanized servants. It accomplished something else too: it put us, as a species, on a collision course with Earth's capacity to maintain life.

Picture the scene. It's summertime on the island of Aegina. Suddenly, three firefighting aeroplanes pass over our house, heading towards the Peloponnese. We look out after them, and there it is in the distance: black smoke, rising over the Parnon mountain range into the sky like a charmed snake, gradually covering the blazing midday sun and creating a strange, dystopic sunset. There's no need to turn on the news to know that a major disaster is unfolding before our eyes. But while our hearts are sinking, in economic terms the health of market society will be rising fast. Not in spite of the forest fire but because of it.

Yes, I know it sounds absurd, but it's true: according to a variety of measures, the economy benefits from our biosphere's suffering. First of all, those burning pine trees had no exchange value just growing on the mountainside. Whatever their experiential value to someone taking a walk in their shade, enjoying the smell of their resin, listening to the music of the breeze in their branches – a value that is incalculable – their exchange value is zero because they are not commodities than can be bought and sold for a profit. In economic terms, no matter how many trees burn, no matter how scorched the landscape gets, no matter how many animals meet a terrible fate in the flames, no exchange value is lost.

On the other hand, the planes flying over our house burn kerosene, fuel with a high exchange value which is now added to the income of the oil company supplying it. The same goes for the diesel consumed by the firefighting trucks rushing towards the blazing forest. And when the time comes to rebuild the homes that burned down or the power lines that suffered damage, the exchange value of the constructors' wages and the materials involved are all additional fuel for the engine of the economy. See the problem?

Humans are predatory animals and we have long had a tendency to hunt the fauna we rely on to extinction. Destruction of our environment is not new either. On Easter Island the only remnants of the island's ancient human inhabitants are the huge statues they left behind before they were forced by famine to abandon it. Logging of the island's trees loosened the soil, causing it to flow into the ocean when it rained, turning the island into a desert. For most of our history, however, such catastrophes were isolated occurrences. Before market societies emerged and matured – before the Great Transformation that brought about the triumph of exchange values over experiential values and led to the Industrial Revolution – Agent Smith's accusation would have been unfounded and unfair.

Take, for example, the Aboriginal Australians, with whom this book began. It's true they eradicated all of the Australian continent's large mammals thousands of years before the British arrived, but they subsequently managed to attain an equilibrium with their environment, protecting the forests and moderating their consumption of fish, birds and plants in order to preserve nature's wealth. Within a hundred years of the arrival of British colonists, however, who enclosed their land, evicted them from it and subjected it to the laws of their market society, three fifths of the forests had been destroyed. Today Australia's land is wounded by mines and eroded by intensive agriculture, its riverbeds dried and filled with salt. The Great Barrier Reef to the continent's north – formerly the world's largest living structure – is now dying.

As the forest fire suggests, a society that prizes exchange value above everything is one that grossly and criminally undervalues the preservation of the environment. If a tree or a microorganism has no exchange value, our market society behaves as if its destruction is meaningless. If exchange value can be derived from its destruction, we can't act fast enough. Why is this?

Idiots: the original meaning

Imagine a river with trout in it. If we catch them all, the trout will disappear for good. If we catch them a few at a time, the trout will last for ever, since they'll spawn year after year. Now let's see what happens if fishing is no longer regulated by the customs and traditions of a community of people that understand the river's delicate equilibrium and is regulated instead by the laws of market society.

Let's say that the exchange value of each trout is five pounds. If each individual fisherman is motivated solely by personal profit, then each of them will continue fishing until the exchange value of the time and labour they spend doing so costs them a bit more than the exchange value they derive from the fish. How might the exchange value of that time be quantified? Suppose that each hour the fisherman spends fishing he loses the ten pounds he'd be able to make by working at a nearby factory. As long as he catches a fraction more than two fish per hour (which he can sell for five pounds each), it's in his best interest to fish trout instead of working at the factory.

As anyone who has gone fishing knows, the number of fish you catch is inversely proportional to the number of other people fishing nearby and the intensity with which each of them fishes. To put it simply, it's much easier to catch fish if you're the only person fishing. You just drop your net in the water and swoop up five or six in a row. But the more you fish and the more fishermen there are, the harder it gets to catch trout because with each successful catch there is one fewer fish available because more of you are chasing after the trout that remain.

If you were to work collectively as a community of, say, a hundred fishermen, you could agree that you'd each only fish one hour per day, catching a total of two hundred trout between you and sharing them – two each, daily. Yet in market societies, each entrepreneurial fisherman is competing against the rest and such agreements go against the spirit (and sometimes even the law) of competition. Even if, over a pint of beer at the local pub, all one hundred of you agree that it is sensible in theory to limit yourselves to one hour of fishing each day, in practice you will be compelled to do so for a second hour – and a third, and a fourth, and a fifth, and so on – for as long as each additional hour nets you at least two extra trout.

At first the total catch may be big, a lot more than two hundred trout. But soon, as the hundred fishermen spend many hours fishing, the trout get scarce, almost disappearing from the river. At some point, to catch two hundred trout between themselves, the fishermen would have to fish all day every day, instead of the one hour it would have taken them had they stuck to their agreement.

If this is not a prime example of orchestrated stupidity I do not know what is. But this is what befalls us when we assume that the profit motive is a natural human trait: it becomes the guiding force for all we do despite the fact that it is a relatively recent invention of market societies. Not only do we run the risk of ending up like Doctor Faustus or Doctor Frankenstein, we also run the risk of repeating the mistakes of the Easter Islanders, only this time on a planetary scale. For the example of the trout is, as you know, the mere tip of the iceberg. In just the same way, industrial conglomerates driven by corporate profit-seeking abuse the environment for as long as polluting and exploiting result in net exchange value, condemning our planet to burn – not in hell but in an oven of our own making.

In ancient Greece a person who refused to think in terms of the common good was called an *idiotis* – a privateer, a person who minded his own business. 'In moderation as a *poietis* [poet], immoderately as an *idiotis*,' the ancient Athenian saying went. In the eighteenth century British scholars with a passion for ancient Greek texts gave the word *idiotis* its current English meaning – a fool. In both these senses our market societies have turned us into idiots.

Can private and planetary interests be wedded?

Most certainly! The Aborigines managed it just fine, collaborating beautifully to sustain themselves without hunting and fishing all day, allowing them to dedicate their free time to ceremony, story-telling, painting and recitals. As individuals, but also as societies that sought to live in harmony with nature, they achieved an authentic well-being that was the envy of many of the Englishmen who encountered them.

Similarly in Europe, despite it being far more densely populated than Australia people managed to give nature the space it needed to survive prior to the emergence of market societies, the commodification of everything, the privatization of common land, the triumph of exchange value over experiential value and the victory of private profit over the notion of the common good. The fact that feudal commons were also the site of insufferable cruelty and prejudice does not diminish the environmental point.

Today, if we are to have any chance of saving the planet and ourselves we must find ingenious ways to reactivate humanity's appreciation for experiential values that no market can even recognize, let alone respect. One solution that has been tried with some success is to place limits on profit-seeking behaviour – in other words, to impose as a legal rule an agreement that, say, no fisherman catches trout for more than one hour per day. In Ecuador for example the constitution has been amended in order to recognize the rainforest's right to protection as if this were an invaluable end in itself, regardless of its exchange value – a first in constitutional history.

Such constraints on owners' activities and taxation of their profits are all very well, but the larger question is: how can we make collective responsibility for the planet's resources an *integral* part of society when land, raw materials and machines are owned by a powerful minority that have decisive influence over the governments that script, administer and police our laws when they are resistant to such laws?

The answer you get to this question depends on the vested interests of the person you ask. If you were to ask a landless worker, they might well reply: the way to put a stop to the owners' control over how the planet's productive forces are used is to put an end to the ownership of land, raw materials and machines itself. Collective responsibility can only be brought about through collective ownership – being governed democratically either at the local level via a cooperative or nationally via the state.

On the other hand, if you ask one of the minority that owns a large amount of land and machines, then you will most likely get a different answer. He will say something like: 'Let's agree that something needs to be done to save the planet. But do you seriously believe the government is an unadulterated expression of our collective interests?

174

No! The government serves the interests of those who run it – politicians and bureaucrats – interests that don't represent the majority of people or the planet at all. As for your romantic idea of a cooperative, have you ever known anything important to have been accomplished democratically, with everyone sitting around, talking incessantly, paralysed by the complexity of it all? No, this is impossible. As Oscar Wilde once said, "The trouble with socialism is that it takes too many evenings."'

If you were then to ask, 'So how do you suggest we save the planet?' his answer would most probably be as follows.

'More markets, please!'

In order to defend their right to own land, machines and resources, defenders of the status quo would say something like: 'Sure, you are right. The reason market society fails to manage the planet's natural resources properly is that these resources have experiential value but no exchange value. The solution is to *give* them exchange value. Take the beautiful forest that is now in flames, causing you such sorrow. Since it belongs to everyone, it belongs to no one. The reason our market society does not value it as much as it should is because nobody can gain exchange value from it. The same goes for the trout in the river. They don't belong to anyone until they are caught, and that's why each fisherman catches as many as they please, the result being that the trout disappear and the fishermen look stupid. The same is true for the atmosphere: it doesn't belong to anyone, and as a result each one of us exploits it until it becomes poisoned. Since cooperative control is unworkable and governmental control is inefficient, biased and authoritarian, I'd suggest the following solution: give all these precious but unpriced natural resources to someone who can make them profitable – me, for example – and then they will certainly be looked after.'

Indeed, it can be argued that if the river and all the trout swimming in it were privately owned, the owner would have every reason to protect them. Perhaps they would charge an entrance fee or an hourly rate to fish the river, ensuring that fishing was limited and thereby protecting both the trout and the fishermen's labour. The same goes for the atmosphere or the forests. If these were privately owned, then industries would be forced to pay for the right to emit pollutants into the air and families would be forced to pay to have a picnic in the forest, ensuring that both were used in moderation while the owner ensured they were protected and sustained.

'How exactly does this differ from feudalism?' you may ask. Back then the land, along with the animals, plants and people that inhabited it, all belonged to some lord. Are we now being told that we need to return to a feudal system to save the planet? Defenders of market societies will answer, 'Not at all. The beauty of a market-based solution is that, irrespective of who is given the natural resources to begin with, once those natural resources are available to be bought and sold they will inevitably end up in the hands of whoever can manage them most profitably and efficiently, for it is they who will be able to pay the most in order to own them. This is completely different from their being controlled indefinitely according to the arbitrary whims of some feudal despot.'

In fact, private ownership need not mean ownership by a single person or corporation. The rivers, forests and atmosphere could just as easily be bought and sold in small pieces by thousands of different owners in markets designed especially for that purpose. And how does one cut up a forest or the planet's atmosphere into separate pieces? By issuing so-called shares in those resources which legally entitle the owner of each share to a proportion of the profits generated by those resources, just as you can own tiny shares in giant companies like Apple or Ford.

It may seem paradoxical to you that preventing the destruction of the environment by market society's preference for exchange value over experiential value should require us to convert every last remaining experiential value into exchange value, but this type of thinking and proposal is currently all the rage.

The irony of market solutions

In fact, this argument for commodifying nature is not a theoretical one. Though its application has so far been moderate and coy, it has been winning debates and shaping what governments and business do for a while now. Instead of privatizing the atmosphere, here is what some governments have done to tackle air pollution.

Every company is given the right to emit a certain amount of noxious gases into the atmosphere, as well as the right to sell that right to other companies. Within this newly created market, companies that manufacture cars, generate energy, fly planes and other activities that involve releasing tons of these gases into the atmosphere can buy the right to emit polluting fumes from those who do not need it – for example, from a company powered by solar panels. The merit of this system, according to its proponents, is twofold.

First, companies that can pollute less than their entitlement have the incentive to do so because the less they pollute, the more money they stand to make from selling their remaining quota. Second, the price a company pays for being allowed to pollute more than its quota is determined by supply and demand in the market, instead of being set by untrustworthy politicians. It sounds pretty smart, doesn't it?

But pay attention to the irony: the only reason to adopt a market solution such as this is because government can't be trusted, and yet this solution depends entirely on the government for it to work. Who decides what the original quota of pollution will be? Who monitors each farmer, fisherman, factory, train or car's emissions? Who fines them if they exceed their quotas? The government of course. Only the state has the ability to create this artificial market because only the state has the power to regulate each and every company.

The reason the rich and powerful, along with their intellectual and ideological supporters, recommend the complete privatization of our environment is not that they are opposed to government; they're just opposed to government interventions that undermine their property rights and threaten to democratize processes that they now control. And if, in the process, they get to own Planet Earth, that's OK by them too!

The only practical solution: authentic democracy

I said that in this book I'd be talking to you about the economy, but you'll have noticed by now that it's impossible to talk about the economy without talking about politics.

At the end of the last chapter I said that you can take the money out of politics but you cannot take the politics out of money; that any attempt to depoliticize the regulation and management of the money supply would choke the economy and prevent recovery in the event of a crash. I concluded that the only solution was to democratize the process by which monetary decisions are made. And at the end of the chapter before that, do you remember asking what can be done in the face of the fierce opposition of the small but powerful minority who own all the machines if we are ever to escape becoming the slaves of our creations? The answer was similar: democratize technology by making all humans the robots' part owners.

Now, in this chapter, I am taking the same line further by arguing that a decent, rational society must democratize not only the management of money and technology, but the management of the planet's resources and ecosystems as well. Why so much emphasis on democracy? Because, to paraphrase Winston Churchill's tongue-in-cheek remark, democracy may be a terrible, terrible form of government – as flawed, fallible, inefficient and corrupt as the people of which it is comprised – but it's better than any of the alternatives.

Your era will be typified by the momentous clash between two opposing proposals: 'Democratize everything!' versus 'Commodify everything!' The proposal favoured by powerful and influential people and institutions is 'Commodify everything!' They want to convince you that the solution to our world's problems is to accelerate and to deepen the commodification of human labour, land, machines and the environment. 'Democratize everything!' is the recommendation that I have been building towards throughout this book. Take your pick. The clash of these two agendas will determine your future well after I am gone. If you wish to have any say in that future, then you and your contemporaries will have to form an opinion on this matter and articulate good arguments with which to win others to your point of view.

I am not going to pretend to be neutral in this clash, so I will say this. Commodification will never work. Markets do a great job when it comes to managing the supply of coffee shops in a city and, more generally, the distribution of goods among buyers with different tastes, just as we saw in Radford's POW camp. But as I have attempted to show over the course of this book, they are *terrible* at managing money, labour and robots. As for the environment, the market solution combines the worst of the market with the drawbacks of state intervention.

'OK,' you will say, 'you reject the *markets-everywhere* solution and propose instead the *democracy-everywhere* alternative. But how on Earth will your democracy save the planet, put the robots to work for us and make money function sensibly and smoothly?' What a great question! While it would take a whole other book to answer it properly, let me offer a hint that may help you write that sequel yourself one day.

In both markets and democracies we vote. In elections the more votes a party or proposition gets, the more it can influence the political outcome. Something similar happens in markets. When you buy a particular ice cream, you are sending a message to the producer of that ice cream that you consider the ice cream sufficiently desirable to spend money on. It's as if you're voting in favour of that particular type of ice cream. If no one buys it, the company will stop producing it. If lots of kids like you vote for it with their pounds and pence, then the company will produce more.

But there is a profound difference between these two kinds of voting. In a democracy we have one single vote each. This is a prerequisite for the Greek concept of *isegoria*: giving different views equal weight. In markets, however, the number of votes one has is determined by one's wealth. The more pounds, euros, dollars or yen you have, the greater the weight of your opinion in the markets where you spend them. It's the same with shares in a company: if you own 51 per cent of the shares in a company, you are its absolute ruler, even if the remaining 49 per cent are owned by thousands of people.

You may well say, 'Given that we all live on the same planet, why would the wealthy want something any less than optimal for Spaceship Earth, since we're all on board together?' Consider this: as humans, we now face the choice of either drastically reducing greenhouse gas emissions or letting the polar ice caps melt, which would cause the sea level to rise, resulting in the loss of millions of people's homes and farms in low-lying coastal areas such as Bangladesh and the Maldives. Now suppose we've privatized the atmosphere, and the decision about what action to take lies in the hands of people whose wealth means they will never be affected by rising sea levels but who will face a reduction in their profits, perhaps even the loss of their jobs or businesses, if they reduce emissions. Is it right, do you think, that they as majority shareholders should make this decision while the people whose houses and farms will disappear under the rising waters should have no say? Do you see why the voting of shareholders will never protect the planet in the same way that democracy could?

The fact that our democracies are imperfect and corrupt doesn't change the fact that democracy remains our only chance to avoid behaving, collectively, like foolish viruses. It is our only hope to prove Agent Smith wrong.

Epilogue

Over the course of this book, while I have been going on and on about the economy, my greatest fear is that all along you've been wondering, *How can Dad have confused me with someone who gives a damn?*

Setting aside my bruised ego, my fear stems from a larger worry: that most people have no time to scrutinize society. We just want to get on with our lives, chat with our mates and enjoy the pleasures that market society provides. Maybe books like this seem at best a distraction or an irrelevance, at worst an obstacle to enjoying life.

I suppose I could respond by arguing that market societies are bad at producing genuine pleasure, that market society is in truth a joyless place. But I won't do so here. Instead, I shall beg for your attention for just a little longer and ask you to participate in a thought experiment.

Escape hatch

Imagine that our friend Kostas, a mad scientist, has designed and built a magnificent computer called

HALPEVAM: Heuristic ALgorithmic Pleasure & Experiential VAlue Maximizer. HALPEVAM is the opposite of the horrible, misanthropic machines in *The Matrix*, which designed a virtual reality in order to help enslave and exploit humanity. In contrast, HALPEVAM is designed to be our faithful servant – the ultimate pleasure machine.

HALPEVAM reads your brainwaves to work out with 100 per cent accuracy what you like and what annoys or saddens you. It then creates for you a virtual life that is *by your own standards* the best of all possible lives, and while in it, you have no clue that it is virtual. Above all, its primary directive is never to change our desires or motives to suit its virtual world but to create a virtual reality in perfect harmony with your own desires, sensitivities, aspirations and principles, just as they are.

Now, suppose that Kostas' birthday present to you next May is a cool-looking marker pen. He tells you that you can use it to draw a large square or circle on any wall, and then, just as Harry Potter and his friends catch the train from Platform 9¾, you can jump through the wall to the other side. What's on the other side?

The other side is the virtual world created by HALPEVAM especially for you. A landscape of unlimited pleasure awaits, with none of the chores, pains and sorrows of normal life, none of the boring tales your dad tells you. While you are immersed in maximum experiential bliss, your body will be cared for in an advanced facility by a team of medical androids who receive their instructions from HALPEVAM, ensuring its tip-top physical condition.

Would you go for it? 'Sure,' I hear you say.

'Not so quick,' Kostas warns. The catch is that if you go through the wall you cannot come back. You will have to live all the rest of your days in the perfect dream world of HALPEVAM.

So here is the question: would you go through the wall *for ever*?

Beyond satisfaction

If you decide that you will not, then you have rejected the notion that the satisfaction of your preferences is all that matters. At the same time, you may find it hard to explain precisely why you feel this way. Perhaps the thought of having to saying goodbye to your current reality, even to your dad, is too much to bear? The prospect of a life of pure bliss is not enough to take away the apprehension that fills your soul at the thought of leaving all *this* behind.

But what if Kostas were to program HALPEVAM to tele-transport you to your virtual bliss without you realizing it? What if the corporation that owns HALPEVAM were to organize this for every human on the planet? None of us would be aware of any difference except a remarkable improvement in our levels of happiness, satisfaction, fulfilment, joy – even while our bodies, along with billions of others, were being looked after by scores of androids designed and directed by HALPEVAM.

Would you describe this as heaven? Or as a hell not substantially different from the one that Neo and his comrades were struggling to escape from in *The Matrix*? If, like me, this image makes you shiver with disgust, then we have just agreed: preference satisfaction is hugely important but it is not everything.

So let's pause for a moment to ask what is *really* wrong with the world HALPEVAM is trying to create for us? What, in other words, is the difference between satisfying our desires and authentic happiness?

Sure, when our desires are fulfilled we feel happy. For a while at least. And that is a good thing. But as John Stuart Mill, a British philosopher and political economist, warned us in 1863, 'It is better to be a human being dissatisfied than a pig satisfied, better to be Socrates dissatisfied than a fool satisfied. And if the fool, or the pig, are of a different opinion, that is because they know only their side of the story.' In other words, ignorance may be bliss – and the bliss that HALPEVAM offers is impossible without it – but authentic happiness requires something more like its opposite.

You see, looking for happiness is not like digging for gold. Gold is defined independently of who we are or, more importantly, who we are becoming by digging for it. There is a chemical test that allows us, or a computer, to establish whether what glitters is truly gold or not. But in the case of authentic happiness there is no such thing. As a result, all that HALPEVAM can do is reflect back at us the preferences we had when we joined it. And yet living a successful life, a life in which authentic happiness is a possibility, is a process of becoming – for which the Greeks had a word, *eudaimonia*, meaning 'flourishing' – in which our character and our thoughts, and thus our preferences and desires, constantly evolve.

Looking at photographs of myself when I was in my late teens or early twenties, I remember the things that I obsessed about then, my preferences and preoccupations, and I cringe. Would I want to live in a universe that constantly served *those* preferences and preoccupations? You bet I wouldn't.

But to what do we owe the evolution of our character and our desires? Conflict is the short answer. Yes, we owe our character to our confrontation with the world and its refusal to grant us all our wishes at once, as well as to the conflict within us made possible by our capacity to think to ourselves, *I want X, but* should *I want X?* We loathe constraints but at the same time understand that they liberate us, if only by helping us question our own motives. Authentic happiness is impossible, in other words, without dissatisfaction as well as satisfaction.

Rather than being enslaved by satisfaction, we need the liberty to be dissatisfied.

These two conflicts, the internal and the external, which depend on liberty and autonomy, are the key to our development. While it may be well intentioned and valiant in its efforts to serve us, HALPEVAM can only encase us in a dystopia, in a tyranny of our own frozen preferences and of a self that cannot grow, develop or transcend itself.

What is the point of any of this in the context of a book on the economy? It is that HALPEVAM is designed to do that which market society strives to accomplish: to satisfy your preferences. Judging by the wholesale unhappiness around us, market society does so terribly incompetently, but the point is that you live in a type of economy that is not only terrible at achieving the goals it sets itself but, far worse, an economy whose goals should *never* be met.

Freedom and the mall

The key to happiness, the American writer Henry David Thoreau once wrote, is not to look for it. It is like a colourful butterfly: 'The more you chase it, the more it will elude you. But if you turn your attention to other things, it will come and sit softly on your shoulder.' So, if happiness is not the goal we should be aiming at, even if we crave it no end, what should be our aims? You must find your own answer, but while you are thinking about it, here are some personal thoughts.

Something that angers and terrifies me more than almost anything else is the thought of being the plaything of forces and people of which I am oblivious. I think most people feel this way. That's why movies like *The Matrix* and *V for Vendetta* have proved so popular: they appeal to our need to be self-directing, autonomous, free thinkers. The worst slavery is that of heavily indoctrinated happy morons who adore their chains and cannot wait to thank their masters for the joy of their subservience.

Our market societies manufacture fantastic machines and incredible wealth, astounding poverty and mountainous debts, but at the same time they manufacture the desires and behaviours required in us for its perpetuation. The perfect example of this is the shopping mall. The architecture, the interior design, the music: everything is designed to numb the mind and marshal us at optimal speed through the aisles and shops, to stifle spontaneity and creativity and instead to manufacture the desire in us to leave its shops burdened with stuff that we probably neither needed nor wanted when we went in. Knowing this, I cannot help but loathe them. Instead, give me HALPEVAM any time, or even the Matrix!

There are other means of indoctrination as well. One is the mass media, whose purpose is also to fabricate mass consent to the oligarchy's political decisions against our own interests and those of the planet. Another is the most potent form of ideological indoctrination of them all: economics.

Ideology

'So, how did these rulers manage to maintain their power, distributing surplus as they pleased, undisturbed by the majority?' This was a question I posed near the beginning of this book, in Chapter 1. My answer was 'By cultivating an ideology which caused the majority to believe deep in their hearts that only their rulers had the right to rule.'

This was so in Mesopotamia and it is so today. Every dominion needs a dominant ideology to legitimize it, a narrative that invokes fundamental ethical values in order to justify itself while threatening punishment for those who doubt in it. Organized religion has provided such narratives for centuries, developing sophisticated superstitions to shore up the power of rulers, justifying their autocratic power – and the violence and theft it allows – as the divinely mandated natural order of things.

As market societies emerged, religion took a back seat. The birth of science that in time made the Industrial Revolution possible also gradually revealed belief in a divine order to be just that: a belief, nothing more. The ruling class needed a new narrative with which to legitimize themselves, and they drew on the same mathematical methods of physicists and engineers to prove, with theorems and equations, that market societies were the ultimate natural order, created as if by an invisible hand, to use the words of their most famous founding father – the economist Adam Smith. This ideology, this new secular religion, was of course economics.

Since the nineteenth century, economists writing books and newspaper articles, now appearing on TV, radio and online, have been the apostles of market society. When normal people hear or read them, they tend to draw this conclusion: *The economy is too technical and boring to bother. I should leave it to the experts.* Except the truth is that there are no real experts, and the economy is too important to leave to the economists. As we have seen in this book, economic decisions decide everything from the mundane to the profound. Leaving the economy to the experts is the equivalent of those who lived in the Middle Ages entrusting their welfare to the theologians, the cardinals and the Spanish inquisitors. It is a terrible idea.

Have I ever told you why I became an economist? Because I refused to leave it to the experts. The more I understood the economists' theories and mathematics the more I realized that the so-called experts in our great universities, on our TV screens, in the banks and finance ministries did not have a clue. The smartest among them created brilliant models that could only be solved mathematically if the reality of labour, money and debt described in this book was first removed from those models, rendering them irrelevant to market societies. The rest, the second-raters among economic commentators, not only did not understand the models of the great economists, whom they worshipped, but remarkably did not seem to care that they did not understand them.

The more I heard these economic experts talk about the economy, the more they sounded like sages or oracles from a pre-modern era. And that was not by chance. In the 1930s the British anthropologist E. E. Evans-Pritchard spent time studying the society of the Azande, an African tribe. While living with them he observed that the Azande placed great store in their oracles, from whom they obtained prophecies just as the ancient Greeks did from the Oracle of Delphi. But since these prophecies often turned out to be completely inaccurate, he wondered how the oracles managed to maintain their unwavering power over the tribe. Evans-Pritchard's explanation for the Azande people's steadfast faith in the infallibility of their oracles went as follows: 'Azande see as well as we that the failure of their oracle to prophesy truly calls for explanation, but so entangled are they in mystical notions that they must make use of them to account for failure. The contradiction between experience and one mystical notion is explained by reference to other mystical notions.'

Today's economic experts are not much different. Whenever they fail to predict properly some economic phenomenon, which is almost always, they account for their failure by appealing to the same mystical economic notions that failed them in the first place. Occasionally new notions are created in order to account for the failure of the earlier ones.

For instance, the notion of 'natural unemployment' was created to explain the failure of market societies to produce full employment and of the experts to explain that failure. More generally, unemployment and low economic activity have been held up as proofs of insufficient competition, to be fought by the magic of 'deregulation' – the releasing of bankers and oligarchs from government restraints. If deregulation does not work, more privatization is thought to be able to do the trick instead. When this fails, it must have been the fault of the labour market, which must be liberated from the interference of trade unions and the impediment of social security benefits. And so it goes on.

How exactly are today's experts any different from the Azande priests?

Theology with equations

Many people will tell you that your father doesn't know what he's talking about; that economics *is* a science. That just as physics uses mathematical models to describe nature, so economics uses mathematical models to reveal the workings of the economy. This is nonsense.

Economists do make use of lovely mathematical models and an army of statistical tools and data. But this does not really make them scientists, at least not in the same way that physicists are scientists. Unlike physics, in which nature is the impartial judge of all predictions, economics can never be subjected to impartial tests. It would be not just hard but impossible to create a laboratory in which economic circumstances can be sufficiently controlled and replicated for any scientific experiment to have validity – to test for example how world history would have evolved if in 1929 the state had printed money to give to the poor instead of opting for austerity, or how Greece would have fared if in 2010 the bankrupt Greek state had refused to take out the largest loan in history on conditions of the most savage austerity ever practised. When economists insist that they too are scientists because they use mathematics, they are no different from astrologists protesting that they are just as scientific as astronomers because they also use computers and complicated charts.

Fellow economists, as you can imagine, get very cross with me when I tell them that we face a choice: we can keep pretending we are scientists, like astrologists do, or admit that we are more like philosophers, who will never know the meaning of life for sure, no matter how wisely and rationally they argue. But were we to confess that we are at best worldly philosophers, it is unlikely we would continue to be so handsomely rewarded by the ruling class of a market society whose legitimacy we provide by pretending to be scientists.

An Archimedean leap

Having rejected the escape offered by Kostas' HALPEVAM, what next for you? The third-rate simulation of HALPEVAM offered by the shopping mall? An insurrection against the status quo? Or a decision to carve out your own niche in our highly imperfect world? You will need to work it out for yourself.

Whatever course you choose, there is something I recommend you take with you: the idea of the ancient scientist Archimedes that, given enough distance, nothing is impossible. 'Give me somewhere to stand, and a lever long enough, and I shall lift the Earth,' he said. All systems of domination work by enveloping us in their narrative and superstitions in such a way that we cannot see beyond them. Taking a step or two back, finding a way to inspect them from the outside, allows us a glimpse of how imperfect, how ludicrous, they are. Securing this glimpse keeps you in touch with reality. This is why (I think) you rejected HALPEVAM's world – because once within it, an Archimedean perspective would be impossible.

Market society also instils illusory beliefs in us, though never as efficiently or happily as HALPEVAM. They thus lead us to behaviours that reinforce it at the expense of our creativity, our relationships, our humanity and of course our planet. Whether you adapt your behaviour to suit market society's needs, or become obstinate enough to want to adapt society to your own ideas about what society should be like instead, performing the Archimedean leap – a periodic mental withdrawal from our society's norms and certainties – is vital.

When you were born, your name, Xenia, appealed to me greatly because its etymology comes from the Greek word *xenos*, meaning 'stranger' or 'foreigner' and translates as 'kindness to strangers'. The appeal of this name came in part from my belief that the best way to see your country, your society, is to see it through the eyes of an outsider, a refugee. Try mentally to travel to a faraway place, if not necessarily in order to move your world – though how splendid that would be! – but to see it clearly for what it is. Doing so will grant you the opportunity to retain your freedom. And to remain a free spirit as you grow up and make your way in this world, it is essential that you cultivate a rare but crucial freedom: the liberty that comes from knowing how the economy works and from the capacity to answer the trillion-dollar question: 'Who does what to whom around your neck of the woods and further afield?'

So, enough! You have suffered me sufficiently. Since we have come full circle, returning to the question of why some have so much while others have so little, you may say I have wasted your time. In reply, I offer only this favourite verse:

> We shall not cease from exploration
> And the end of all our exploring
> Will be to arrive where we started
> And know the place for the first time.

Index

Aboriginal Australians,
     8–9, 12, 13, 18, 19–20,
     92, 169, 173
accounting, 13
Achilles, 36–8
Adults in the Room, 3
Aegina, 3, 4, 27
Africa, 21
Agamemnon, 35–6
agoranomy, 35, 38
agriculture
     commodification, 33–4
     surplus, 11–22
Ajax, 36–8
Amazon, 10, 28, 124
Amsterdam, Netherlands,
     110
Apple, 10, 28, 117, 122, 124,
     177
arbitrage, 136–9
Archimedes, 197
Aristotle, 123
armies, 16
artificial intelligence, 107

assembly lines, 121
Athens, 5, 149, 172
Attwood, Margaret, 5
Australia
     Aborigines, 8–9, 12, 13,
          18, 19–20, 92, 169, 173
     environment, 169, 173
     Great Depression
          (1929–39), 65
     Reserve Bank, 75
     unemployment, 91
automation, 107, 116–33
Azande, 194

bacteria, 18–19
Bangladesh, 120–21, 182
Bank of England, 75
banking, 65–89
     crashes, 70–89, 100, 130
     money, creation of,
          68–89, 151–6
     and state, 74–89
bankruptcy, 79–82, 130
biochemical war, 19, 20

Birmingham, England, 84

Bitcoin, 157–62

Blade Runner, 114, 125–7, 129

Blake, William, 46

blood market, 5, 30–31

Bloomberg screens, 139

Bombay, India, 41

bonds, 87

boomerangs, 18

Brecht, Berthold, 5

Brexit, 4

Britain, *see under* United Kingdom

Brothers Grimm, 51, 114

bureaucracy, 16

Byron, George Gordon, 109

capital goods, 38

capitalism, 4

Catholicism, 61–2

central banks, 74–7, 88, 100, 152, 155–6

Chaplin, Charlie, 121

China, 21, 37, 40, 45, 122

cholera, 19, 109

Christianity, 60–62, 165

Christmas Carol, A (Dickens), 62–3, 129

Churchill, Winston, 180

cigarettes, 139–48, 152–6, 162

Clyde river, 48

coal mining, 48

commodities, 28–49

compass, 40

Cornwall, England, 48

counterfeit coins, 149–50

credit, 15

crises, economic, *see* economic crises

currency, 14–15, 77, 139–63

cigarettes as, 139–48, 152–6, 162

counterfeit, 149–50

digital, 156–62

metal, 14, 15, 148, 149

v. money, 153–6

shells as, 14, 15, 77, 148, 149

trust in, 148–50

debt, 5, 13–16, 51–63, 100–102, 154

banking, 65–89

defaulting, 141

exchange value, loan of, 67–70

money market, 100–102

public, 85–9, 151, 154

redemption, 60

writing off, 79–82
debtors' prisons, 80
deflation, 142–6, 160–61
democracy
    and automation, 130–33,
        180
    and economic
        knowledge, 2
    and environment, 179–83
    and money, 162
deregulation, 195
Diamond, Jared, 5
Dickens, Charles, 62–3
digital currency, 156–62
disease, 18–19, 109, 128,
    165–7, 183
Doctor Faustus (Marlowe),
    51–4, 56, 59–61, 111,
    166, 172

Easter Island, 168–9, 172
economic crises, 70–89,
    100, 129–30, 156
    global financial crisis
        (2008–), 100, 130, 156
    Great Depression
        (1929–39), 65–6, 81,
        100, 196
    Greek debt crisis
        (2009–), 65, 80, 81,
        91, 196

economics, ideology of,
    192–7
economy, etymology of,
    32, 33
Ecuador, 173–4
Egypt, ancient, 18,
    111–12
enclosures, 42–4, 54–5,
    83–4
England, 40–44, 48, 54–5,
    120; *see also* United
    Kingdom
environment, 165–83
equilbrum, 138
eudaimonia, 189
Eurasia, 19–21
European Central Bank,
    75
Evans-Pritchard, Edward
    Evan, 194
exchange value, 29–38,
    47–8, 53, 61, 67,
    96–7, 167
    of environment, 167–83
    loaning of, 67–70
    of money, 141, 142–4,
        145
    and technology, 122,
        124–8
experiential value, 30–38,
    47–8, 52, 96–7

of environment, 167,
168, 169, 173, 177
extinction, 166, 168

factories, 39, 43, 45–7, 48,
58, 113, 120–21
fallacy of composition, 5
Faust (Goethe), 59–62
Federal Reserve, 75
Ferrari, 96
feudalism, 32, 39, 41–57,
176–7
flu, 19, 109
Ford, 177
France, 135–9
Frankenstein (Shelley),
109–14, 116, 120, 128,
166, 172

G20, 156
Geneva Conventions,
135
geography, 19–22
Germany, 135–48, 152–6
ghost in the machine,
88–9, 154
Gift Relationship, The
(Titmuss), 5
global financial crisis
(2008–), 100, 130, 156
global trade, 40–44

von Goethe, Johann
Wolfgang, 59–62, 114
gold, 148, 188–9
Gold Standard, 161–2
goods, 28–40
Google, 124
Grapes of Wrath, The
(Steinbeck), 65–6, 81
Great Barrier Reef, 169
Great Contradiction, 47–8
Great Depression (1929–
39), 65–6, 81, 100,
196
Great Need, 91
Great Reversal, 54–7, 61,
106
Great Transformation
(Polanyi), 5
Great Transformation, 40,
130–33, 169
Greece
Civil War (1946–9),
162–3
debt crisis (2009–), 65,
80, 81, 91, 196
mythology, 35–6, 102–5,
116–20
Oracle of Delphi, 194
Grexit, 4
Guns, Steel and Germs
(Diamond), 5

HALPEVAM, 186–90, 197–8
Hammond, Will, 3
Harry Potter (Rowling), 186
Heilbroner, Robert, 5
Hephaestus, 36
Homer, 35–8
housing, 73–4, 91–3, 96

Icarus, 116–20, 122
ideology, 17–18, 24, 192–5
idiotis, 172
Ikaria, 162
Inca civilisation, 18
India, 41
Industrial Revolution, 45–7, 58, 61, 70, 169, 192
inequality, 7–25
    and geography, 19–22
    and Industrial Revolution, 47–8
    and oligarchy, 22–3
    and religion, 17–18
inflation, 142–6, 150
intellectual property, 122
interest, 52, 60–63, 66, 70, 71, 101, 144–6
Internet, 10, 157
iPad, 10, 28

iPhone, 117, 122
Iraq, 13
isegoria, 182
Islam, 60, 165

Jamaica, 48
Japan, 41
Judaism, 135, 165

Keynes, John Maynard, 5, 132
Kostas, Captain, 27–9, 31, 52

labour market, 39, 40, 42–4, 47, 58, 61, 91–107, 195
    automation, 116–33
    unemployment, 91–100
London, England, 84
Luddites, 120

machines, 112–33
Makronissos, 162
Maldives, 182
Manchester, England, 48, 84
Marathonas Beach, 27
market price, 29–38
market society, 4, 10, 27–48, 110

and environment,
167–83
exchange v. experiential
value, 29–38, 47–8,
52–3, 96–7, 167, 169,
173
genesis of, 38–48
ideology of, 192–5
labour market, 39, 40,
42–4, 47, 58, 61,
91–107, 116–33
money market, 100–107,
142–63
and technology, 107,
112–33
Marlowe, Christopher,
51–4, 56, 59–61, 111,
166, 172
Marx, Karl, 5, 116, 117, 121
Mastercard, 157
mathematical models,
195–6
Matrix, The, 114–16, 122,
127–9, 165–6, 183,
188, 191
mechanization, 107, 112–33
Melanesia, 37
Mephistopheles, 51–4,
59–62, 111
Mesopotamia, 13, 77, 149,
192

metal currency, 14, 15, 148,
149
Microsoft, 124
Midas, 119
Mill, John Stuart, 188
Modern Times, 121
Moe, Jacob, 3
money
creation of, 68–89,
151–6
v. currency, 153–6
democratization
of, 162
market, 100–107, 142–63
origin of, 14
as political, 148–63

Nakamoto, Satoshi, 157–8
Napoleonic wars (1803–
15), 110
natural unemployment,
195
Nazi Germany (1933–45),
135–48, 152–6
Netherlands, 40, 110
New Deal, 161

Odysseus, 36–8
Oedipus, 102–5
oikonomia, 32, 33
oligarchy, 22–3, 192

optimism v. pessimism, 93–106
oracles, 194
Ovid, 36

Parthenon, Athens, 18
Patmos, 91, 92, 96
Payback (Attwood), 5
Peloponnese Mountains, 3, 27
pessimism v. optimism, 93–106
Phoenicia, 37
Plato, 123
poietis, 172
Polanyi, Karl, 5
police, 16
political money, 148–63
pollution, 178–9
Portugal, 40
power of prophecy, 103–5
prisoners of war (POWs), 135–48, 152–6, 181
production process, 38–40
automation of, 116–33
profit, 52–63, 73, 111–12
property rights, 16
prophecy, power of, 103–5
Protestantism, 61–2
public debt, 85–9, 151, 154
Pyramids, 18

Radford, Richard, 135–48, 152–6, 181
recycling, 65–89
Red Cross, 135–48, 152–6
redemption, 60
religion, 16–18, 24, 60–62, 165, 192
Reserve Bank, 75
Romanticism, 111
Rome, ancient, 36, 151
Roosevelt, Franklin Delano, 161
Rousseau, Jean-Jacques, 93–5, 99, 102, 146
rule of law, 151

Sahara Desert, 21
science, 1
Scotland, 40, 48
Second World War (1939–45), 135–48, 152–6
Shanghai, China, 40
Shelley, Mary, 109–14, 116, 120, 128, 166, 172
shells, 14, 15, 77, 148, 149
shipbuilding, 40, 48
shopping malls, 191
silk, 40
Singapore, 86
Sisyphus, 119

slavery, 18, 32, 39, 45, 48, 112
smallpox, 19
Smith, Adam, 193
socialism, 175
Socrates, 123, 188
solar panels, 178
Sophocles, 102–5
Sorcerer's Apprentice, The
    (Goethe), 114
Spain, 40
speech, 11
spices, 41
spread, 137
stag hunt, 93–5, 99, 102, 146
Star Trek, 112, 122, 124,
    129, 132
state, 16–18, 20, 24
    and banking, 74–89, 101
    and environmental
        regulation, 178–9
    and ideology, 17–18, 24,
        192
    and money, 148–63
    and surplus, 16–18, 20
    and taxation, 83–7,
        151–2, 154
steam engines, 45, 46, 58, 111
Steinbeck, John, 65–6, 81
surplus, 12–25
    and disease, 18–19
    Great Reversal, 54–7, 61

and ideology, 17–18, 24,
    192
and oligarchy, 22–3
and state, 16–18, 20
and technology, 18, 20
sweatshops, 121
Sweet Porridge (Brothers
    Grimm), 114
swords, 41
Syria, 13

taxation, 83–7, 151–2, 154
technology, 18, 20, 111–33
Terminator, The, 114
Tesla, 124
Thailand, 9
Thoreau, Henry, 190
tin mining, 48
Titmuss, Richard, 5
tomatoes, 96
trade unions, 98–9, 195
Trojan War, 35
trout, 170–72, 175–6
Trump, Donald, 4
typhus, 19

unemployment, 91–100,
    195
United Kingdom
    Australia, colonisation
        of, 8–9, 19–20

Bank of England, 75
Brexit, 4
debtors' prisons, 80
enclosures, 42–4, 54–5, 83–4
feudalism, 41–4, 45–6
global trade, 40–44
Gold Standard, 161
Great Depression (1929–39), 65
Great Reversal, 54–7, 61, 106
Industrial Revolution, 45–7, 58, 110
Luddites, 120
Second World War (1939–45), 135–48, 152–6
slavery, 45, 48
United States
    Federal Reserve, 75
    Gold Standard, 161–2
    Great Depression (1929–39), 65–6, 196
    science, war on, 1
    Trump administration (2017–), 4

usury, 60, 66

V for Vendetta, 191
Vietnam, 21
virtual currency, 14–15
viruses, 165–7, 183
Visa, 157

Wales, 48
Watt, James, 45, 46, 58, 111
welfare state, 151
Wilde, Oscar, 31, 175
women's rights, 32
wool, 40, 41, 43–4, 54–5, 66–7
Worldly Philosophers, The (Heilbroner), 5
writing, 13

xenos, 198

Yokohama, Japan, 41
Yorkshire, England, 48

Zeus, 119
Zimbabwe, 21